YOUR FREE BONUSES
ARE WAITING

Access three bonus tools to deepen your understanding and practice of the **Dear Family Framework.**

Bonus 1: A Closer Look at the Dear Family Framework
(Video Training)
Bonus 2: 7-Day Detox Journal
Bonus 3: Serenity Prayer Exercise

Access your bonuses here:

https://www.tippingpointrecovery.com/get-bonuses/

A PROVEN, REAL-WORLD APPROACH TO HELPING THE ADDICTED FIND LASTING RECOVERY

DEAR FAMILY,

WHY YOUR LOVED ONE WON'T ACCEPT HELP
AND HOW TO HELP THEM ANYWAY

KATE DUFFY

Cover designed by MiblArt.

Paperback ISBN-13: 979-8-9902491-0-3

This book is dedicated to Jonathan.
How I wish we knew then what we know now.

To Laura, Michael, and Jenny.
For the courage, tenacity, and love that fueled you to
confront me with your truth.
I love you.

To Erik and Samantha,
and all those gone far too soon.

To the families who have
trusted me to guide them to become
stronger than the addiction.

To all those sick and suffering.
This book is for you.
It is my hope that it reaches your family.

CONTENTS

ACKNOWLEDGEMENTS

No one recovers alone, and the same goes for the creation of Tipping Point Recovery and the Dear Family Framework. So many people supported me in the writing of this book.

To Laura, Mike, and Jenny. First and foremost, I'm sorry there was not a book and program like this when I was lying to you, hiding from you, and hurting you. Thank you for your courage in standing up to my addiction, for your unconditional love of me and of us, and for your patience with my endless need to talk about recovery!

To Ryan, my best travel buddy. I'm so glad you missed the mess. Thank you for raising your hand in fifth grade to tell your class your nana is sober.

To my family, thank you for loving me unconditionally even when and especially when I was unkind and unwell. For reading what I write and for listening to my shares—even when they are hard to hear. I love you all so much.

To the team who helped me turn my message into an actual book: Laura Speers, my right hand. When you came along as my new VA, neither of us knew what I needed for help or where our working relationship would go. How blessed I am to discover you are the perfect pen for my words. This would never have happened without you. Tina Konstant, Kim Jacobson, and Trevin Jacobson, thank you so much for your editorial feedback, guidance, and cheerful encouragement. We did it.

To my teachers. When I got sober and began working in the field of addiction recovery, I immediately saw the gaping cracks in the systems and often wondered, how is it possible that they discharge us when we say we don't want help? That is simply not true. While I had strong conviction in what I wanted to do, I lacked the confidence and internal self-trust to fully step into the role the Universe was clearly pointing me to. To say mentorship was essential for me is an understatement. The guidance, care, and patience of three people in particular was paramount to me gaining the internal confidence that my external drive was urging me to do. Mike Wilson, Earl Hightower, and Tommy Rosen. Thank you for your endless wisdom and support.

The Worcester County Overdose Response Initiative. To District Attorney Joseph Early, Dr. Patrice Muchowski, and Chief Ernie Martineau, where it all began, thank you for creating a program that so many need. Most especially for putting me at an intersection where a recovery tipping point can occur.

To my faith—for without it I would not have heard the memos or seen the clear path that was being laid out for me. To my peers and teachers at the Rhys Thomas Institute who assisted in the dismantling and rebuilding of my false self to true self.

To the early readers and supporters of this message—Kim Ready, Meg Bartlett, Barbara Rosengren, Dennis Corain, Mike Wilson, Earl Hightower, and Jeff Shearer.

To the mess. I truly thank my addiction and my trauma. I would not be who I am without it all.

To AA, you loved me until I could love myself. The Plymouth House, my recovery doula.

Lastly and most importantly, to all the brave ones. The family recovery warriors and Recovery Conversations families of Fitchburg, Massachusetts and Zoom. You are truly so brave to pull up a chair at the table you never wanted to be at and were so afraid to sit at. You really rolled up your sleeves.

To you all, I ooze gratitude.

We've only just begun.

AUTHOR'S NOTE

On Language

There is a variety of language used to talk about addiction—disease, disorder, condition, illness, etc. Each of them comes with their own nuance and connotation, and opinions differ on which one is best to use. The CDC and National Institute on Drug Abuse categorize substance use disorder (SUD) as a chronic but treatable disease. Alcoholics Anonymous (AA) and similar fellowships teach a threefold disease model. Others argue that addiction does not meet the criteria to be a disease and feel it should be described differently.

In my opinion, none of these terms are perfect, but they do each bring something helpful to the discussion around understanding addiction, and I use them interchangeably throughout this book. I recovered with the support of AA, and so the disease model resonates strongly for me. I also see validity to the arguments against it. To me, what is most important is that the language used around addiction distinguishes it from a moral failing.

In AA when going through the steps, it is suggested to replace the word "God" with a higher power of your understanding. I encourage you to do something similar as you read this book when it comes to how you refer to addiction. If you don't like a word I've used to refer to addiction, you can replace that word with whichever resonates more for you. Ultimately, we can likely all agree that addiction is complex, chronic, and progressive.

On Blame

This book is in no way intended to place blame on the family for their loved one's addiction or imply their recovery is your responsibility. Sometimes the messages I share may feel harsh or like they're insinuating that you are not doing enough. That is far from the truth. This book is intended to shine a light where you may not have otherwise looked. Living alongside addiction is painful, scary, traumatizing, and maddening, and I honor you in seeking alternative ways to approach this.

On Safety

The information shared in this book is intended to be for educational purposes only and should not be taken as professional advice. Each person's and family's situation is unique, and your physical safety is paramount. This is nuanced work, and it is strongly recommended that you consult with a professional for guidance on how to handle your specific situation.

INTRODUCTION
THIS BOOK IS A TIPPING POINT

If you are reading this book, chances are someone dear to you is in the grips of a substance use disorder, which means your world is upside down.

Let me first say this: I see you.

I know the burden you carry.

I know the pain, frustration, and worry you feel.

I know how hopeless this may all seem.

I know because I've been there, on all sides of the table. I am the addict. I am the family member. I am the treatment provider. And the very first thing I want to tell you before anything else is the one thing I am certain your loved one wants you to know:

"I love you, and I'm sorry."

You might question whether your loved one feels this way, but I assure you they do. Every addict and person in recovery I've ever spoken with, including myself, felt that way while they were active in their addiction. We just couldn't say it.

So I'm saying it now, along with the truth I wish someone had told my kids when I was caught in the grips of my own drinking. Here it is:

Your loved one is sick.

They are self-medicating an inside problem. They have developed a chronic, complex, and progressive disorder, and they need treatment.

It is not your fault. You didn't cause this, but there is a way you can help them, and I'm here to show you what it is.

So, that's what I'm doing with this book:

1. Shedding light on the truth about addiction so that you'll stop expecting your loved one to do things their addiction is preventing them from being able to do.

2. Showing you how to get yourself out of the chaos and onto a path that will improve your life *and* dramatically improve the chances of your loved one finding lasting recovery.

I've laid out that path in this book, and here's how it is structured:

First, I'll need you to face some ugly truths about your current reality with addiction. I should warn you that in order to do that, I'm not holding back. I will be fully transparent, honest, and blunt with you on these pages so much so that there may be moments where you get upset at me. (*Sorry, not sorry.*) The more honest you can be with yourself about the ugly stuff, the better equipped you'll be to change it.

After that, I'll share exactly what makes this process so effective and cover the three components that are the key to its—and your—success.

We'll take a look at what's not working when dealing with addiction as well as discuss a few of the most common objections I get when I talk to families about **The Dear Family Framework.**

Next, we'll dive into the framework itself, which is the foundation of all of Tipping Point's family recovery programs, from top to bottom. This process has helped hundreds of families get their loved ones sober and find a lasting path to recovery. I want as many people as possible to know it and use it.

Lastly, I'll focus some time on discussing a widely misunderstood recovery tool: interventions. I'll cover what they are and the process involved in a Tipping Point Recovery™ intervention, and I'll break down why they are even more effective when done alongside our family recovery framework outlined in this book.

You've already got a lot going on, so I'm going to keep things as straightforward and easy to implement as possible. To that end, the core of this book can be summed up in three points:

Point #1: Addiction is a complex and progressive disorder that affects not just the person with the addiction but everyone around them.

Point #2: Families are intricately tied to their loved ones, no matter how their family system is structured, and as such, their loved ones' addictions impact them in significant ways, often throwing them into chaos and strain.

Point #3: Just as addiction is contagious, so is recovery, and families have the power to inspire and initiate the potential for recovery in their loved ones and reclaim peace in their own lives by putting into practice the very framework laid out in this book. I call it **The Dear Family Framework**.

My goal in simplest terms is for you, your loved one, and your family to recover and heal.

I don't just believe, I *know* that together with this framework, we can create a paradigm shift in how the world treats addiction. But it means being willing to do things differently.

This is a Tipping Point.

I hope you choose to take the plunge.

And if after reading this book you want support and guidance to implement this framework in your own life, schedule a time to connect with my team here:

https://tippingpointrecovery.as.me/connection-call

Helping families get their loved ones on a path to recovery and reclaim their own lives in the process is exactly what me and my team do every single day.

To doing things differently,

Kate

PART
01

TIME TO GET HONEST

CHAPTER 1
REALITY CHECK

IMAGINE THIS:

The phone rings. You don't jump at the sound, try to anticipate what might be wrong, or immediately think the worst. No pit forms in your stomach, twisted with dread. You just answer it.

It's your loved one calling to check in on you. It's been a week or two since you last spoke, and they wanted to connect.

You talk for a half hour about the changes at your job, their plans for the weekend, and the movie you recently saw. No one yells. You don't go into "fixer" mode. You don't question if they are telling you the truth. You share what's going on with you, and they share what's going on with them. Some of it good, some of it not so good.

Calm.

They seem happy and engaged the entire conversation, and when you hang up, you go back to whatever it was you were doing before they called, content and at peace, and you realize you are happy too.

It's how you feel most of the time now. You sing in the car on your drive home from work again the way you had years ago before addiction took control. You go for walks in nature. You make the time for the things that feed your soul.

Other people have noticed a change in you too. That you smile more. You don't blow up at others the way you used to. You can have fun again without stressing about when the other shoe will drop.

And when something does come up, whether it's a true crisis or something that would have *felt* like a crisis before, it doesn't send you spiraling. You are grounded, have self-trust, and have a plan to fall back on for just these moments. You have tools to use and skills you've developed to help you navigate challenging situations. You have a community to lean on and turn to for support, strength, and guidance.

If your loved one is active in their addiction, what I've just described might sound like a fantasy. I'm here to tell you that not only is it possible but it's the very real result we've helped hundreds of families turn into reality through **The Dear Family Framework.**

As a result of this framework, our clients reconnect with their loved ones, find and continually strengthen their voices, reclaim their own sense of inner peace, and heal. You see, this book you're reading is more than just a list of recovery tips. It's a way of life, a methodology, that has developed organically from over a decade of my own recovery journey, conversations with thousands of fellow addicts, and my work with hundreds of families on all sides of the treatment system as well as the treatment centers we serve. When put into practice, it's a framework that makes it nearly impossible for addiction to thrive.

Don't just take my word for it. Our client's transformations speak for themselves.

Here are five examples from clients we've served of how **The Dear Family Framework** can bring you peace and help your family recover:

Client Case Study #1: Wife Linda Fired Herself from Being Case Manager

Linda came to us like so many of our families do:

* ❖ Defeated
* ❖ Fed up
* ❖ Convinced she had tried everything she could to get her husband sober

All of her time and energy was spent trying to manage her husband's addiction on top of working a full-time job and caring for their young child. She was constantly checking her husband's phone, looking at his Uber app to try and figure out if he'd been drinking. She would lie for him, covering for him with his boss or his buddies, making excuses for why he didn't show up for a shift or the plans they'd made.

This kind of covering up and hiding is really common. It makes sense why family would do this. Sometimes we don't feel equipped to face the truth. We may not trust what will happen if we address it head on, or we are unsure we can handle the ramifications of shining a light on the problem. Asking for help is super hard, and we often don't know who to even ask. Change is so scary; there's always the fear it will be a change for the worse.

Linda continued to hide her husband's drinking from everyone until she finally told her daycare provider what was going on to explain why she'd need to leave their child at daycare as long as possible each day. It turned out, the daycare provider's boyfriend was a recovering addict, one whose family I'd worked with to help him get sober. She gave Linda my number, and Linda reached out to me.

We ended up intervening on Linda's husband, and while he was in treatment, Linda and her mother-in-law joined our 12-week program followed by time in our year-long family recovery membership.

While in our program, Linda learned the complex layers of addiction, for both herself and her husband, and she quickly fired herself from being his case manager. Rather than try to solve his problems for him, she learned to focus on finding her own peace and groundedness while supporting her husband to find and access professional case managers and treatment professionals who were more qualified to help him.

Years later, Linda has found peace, her husband now works in the field of recovery, and they have a growing family built on healthy boundaries, communication, and transparent recovery.

Client Case Study #2: Mom Jillian Accepted She Didn't Have All the Answers

Jillian had a long history of addiction in her family, including herself. This is not uncommon as children of alcoholics are more likely to become alcoholics themselves. Jillian managed to find her own recovery long before working with us at Tipping Point Recovery, but it was her twenty-year-old son who was struggling when she found us.

He was living at home, basically withering away in his room. No friends, no social life, no real interest in anything. He had become a shell of a person.

At first, Jillian was hesitant to accept outside help. She figured that because of her own experience with recovery, she should know what to do, what it would take, and that she should be able to help her son on her own. But a friend of hers suggested she attend one of our webinars, and something about what I said resonated with Jillian in a way she didn't expect.

After joining our 12-week program, Jillian decided to hire us to intervene on her son, and we got him into a treatment program that met his specific needs. It was during the intervention process that Jillian saw her son come back to life. He connected with others his age in treatment. He'd call her just to check in. He was more like the happy boy he used to be growing up. The treatment program he was in even referred to him as the "Miracle Boy," noting the extreme change they saw in him with the help of the work Jillian was doing with Tipping Point.

Her son wasn't the only one who transformed. Jillian found herself again over the course of our programs, unaware she had even become lost. She was able to go deeper into her own recovery and heal some of the deep-seated wounds she hadn't realized still lingered within herself.

Above all, she realized her son's path was different from her own and, while she could help lead him *to* his path, it wasn't up to her to forge his path for him. Now, they're able to walk side-by-side on their own recovery paths together.

Client Case Study #3: Wife Stacy Stopped Letting Addiction Call the Shots

Stacy came to us much like Linda did: an overwhelmed mother of young children who was trying to keep everything together by herself—work, home, childcare—while also desperately trying to manage her husband's alcoholism, including hiding it from everyone. He had progressed deep into his addiction, and she was just as deeply entrenched in her ways of responding to him, to the point where she was no longer sleeping, had trouble focusing at work, and even started to break out in hives. When her husband's health took a turn for the worse as a result of his drinking, she knew something had to change.

Through the encouragement of her mother and mother-in-law, Stacy joined our 12-week program and immersed herself in the material. She showed up, eager to learn how to start setting healthy boundaries, which were only strengthened once we began an intervention process.

Like most families who choose to do an intervention, Stacy's first response to working with a professional interventionist was one of worry and doubt. She worried that her husband would react poorly and angrily. She feared he'd want a divorce, and that fear sometimes caused her to be less firm in her boundaries.

But she continued to learn the importance of putting his wellness and recovery ahead of his feelings about what she was doing in response to his addiction. She learned to put her boundaries, what she expected for behavior and conduct in her home and around her children, ahead of his feelings as well. She relied on the advice and guidance of our expert team (along with the powerful support of our community of families) rather than let her husband's behaviors continue to call the shots.

All of which led to her finding her voice again. Not only did Stacy's own health improve as her anxiety lessened but her day-to-day life grew more peaceful. As she continued down a recovery path—which included relapses and setbacks—by getting her own sponsor, doing step work, and finding a therapist, her husband gradually got to a place where he became more willing to accept help and take his recovery seriously. Like Stacy, he put tools in place to help himself and engaged in his own recovery community to support him on his path.

Client Case Study #4: Mom Jane and Sister Lana Changed How They Reacted to the Addiction

Lana came to us terrified for her brother and desperate for a way to help him. His addiction was adding drama, chaos, and stress to her family's lives, creating conflict between her and her husband and tension with other family members. She was so relieved when she found us and heard our message that she scoured our website to read and watch as much information as we had available, and she soon reached out to me to learn about joining our 12-week program.

While Lana was all in, her mother Jane was less open to it. She didn't see why she should join a program and do the work when it was her son who had the problem. Lana basically dragged Jane on the initial Zoom call with me, and after speaking with me about our framework, Jane had a pivotal moment. She said, "For years everyone's been telling me to go to a meeting, and I wondered—*why do I have to go to a meeting*?! You just changed that. I see it now. I do have a problem. I don't know what to do, and I do need help."

Gradually over the twelve weeks, Jane discovered that what she *did* have a problem with was her response to her son, her anger, and that her life had become about managing her son. Her son's addiction had impacted her in ways she hadn't even realized, and the way she reacted to it added to the chaos.

Both she and Lana started doing what I suggested. They shared their loved ones' text messages in our private community so I could give them feedback on how to respond in a way that connected, and they used the phrases I gave them in conversations with their loved ones.

The change was undeniable.

The screaming matches stopped. Lana felt connected to her brother again, and even her husband started showing an interest in the recovery work she was doing. People noticed the change in Jane as well. They saw she was calmer and less likely to blow up at people; she was more peaceful. As for Lana's brother, he is now sober, and he and his girlfriend have twin baby girls.

Client Case Study #5: Wife Lizzie Found Her Inner Strength

Lizzie's story is inspiring for the way her relationship improved not just with her husband but with herself as well.

She came to us as a timid and shy woman, reporting low self-esteem. She said she had no hope of her husband ever stopping drinking and figured she just needed to come up with some way to deal with it that would protect her three kids.

Lizzie found Tipping Point Recovery when her husband heard about it after an AA meeting. She continued to work with us for years, enrolling in our 12-week program, doing an intervention, and then continuing on in our year-long membership. To watch her transformation was truly incredible.

The timid, shy person she used to be gradually built up to become a fierce and confident recovery badass. She started to stand up for herself and her needs, no longer accepting just any outcome. She demanded answers to her questions, calling up insurance companies and treatment programs to get the truth she knew she wouldn't get from her husband while he was sick. She put her kids first.

She didn't give up through Covid, an intervention, and the over twenty rounds of detox and treatment centers it took for her husband to find lasting recovery. Each trial and relapse became an opportunity that Lizzie took to learn more about herself and put her recovery tools to work, and her family is stronger for it. Her kids don't cry about their father anymore. Her husband is working his own recovery program, and Lizzie is continuing as an ambassador in ours.

Names of clients and their loved ones have been changed to protect their privacy. For those wanting to hear testimonials directly from our clients themselves, you can do so at: https://www.tippingpointrecovery.com/client-stories/

THE FREEDOM OF FAMILY RECOVERY

As you can see, family recovery doesn't just benefit one or the other, the family or your loved one. Through this framework, the entire family system can recover one person at a time, and it is that community with one another, that culture of recovery, that allows long-term healing to take place.

That healing neither starts nor ends with your loved one. In fact, even if recovery eludes your loved one, you can grow stronger than your pain, fear, and anger, become stronger than the addiction, gain confidence in your choices and decisions, and find peace.

It reminds me of a young man I worked with years ago whose family was fractured when I met them. Erik was a young man struggling with addiction, and his mom was doing everything she could think of to try to help him. I first met them both in the emergency room as they were discussing the possibility of him going to treatment. His mom describes the moment of me walking into the room as an angel being sent to her because she was in such need of help to know what to do, what to say to her son, and how to navigate the treatment system.

While Erik's willingness to go to treatment took some time, I continued to support him and his mom. She was going through a lot. Her siblings were upset with her, accusing her of enabling in the ways she was trying to help her son. Of course they wanted him to get better, too, but they didn't want their sister to be dragged down in the process. They could see her getting swallowed up in her obsession to save him, and it scared them. This kind of fear often manifests in families through arguments, disconnection, and even people no longer speaking to each other.

For over two years, both of Erik's parents, their spouses, and his grandparents attended our weekly support and education group. This family learned about addiction, learned the ways their responses to it had been unhelpful, and began to learn how to support Erik's recovery only. To say it as my colleague and mentor Earl Hightower says, they learned to love him unconditionally and to support him conditionally. I even met several of his aunts and uncles as we intervened one day in the ER. Erik eventually found recovery, and his family repaired, gaining understanding of addiction as well as each other along the way.

A year and a half into sobriety, Erik was thriving and happy in a quality sober house. He and I had been texting to arrange for him to speak in our family program. He was so proud of his recovery.

One day, I received a shocking and devastating call from his mom that he had passed away in his sleep in his sober house.

I attended his wake, and I'll never forget what I saw and felt. This family I had grown so connected to, as devastated as they all were by their untimely loss, had a sense of repair from the initial fractures I witnessed when meeting them. They were on speaking terms. There was love. They understood each other. They supported each other. They had learned that what Erik did was not who he was, and they celebrated him for the person he truly was, not the addiction he had struggled with.

I believe they knew they had done everything they could to help him and themselves.

In all their sadness, it was clear how much more whole and connected the family had grown over the years since I'd met them. I remember thinking as I drove away, *that's a recovering family*.

That's the freedom you can achieve for yourself through this framework. The freedom that only a family who feels they've done everything they could to help their loved one in spite of tragic events could achieve.

As I drove home that night, I cried and talked to Erik. At the time, while I was confident what we had created could help thousands, I was terrified to fully step into this work because of my own fears and insecurities. My ego whispered, "Who the hell are you to do this?" Driving home from the wake, I promised Erik I would bring this work to as many families as I could.

The truth is, I can't guarantee your loved one's recovery. No one can. What I *can* guarantee is you don't have to get shredded up alongside them (like my family did). I *can* guarantee your loved one will have an exponentially better chance of recovery when you recover, too, and I can teach you new ways of responding to and understanding your loved one so you and your family can start to repair the same way Erik's did.

Because in the end, your loved one and the connection you have to each other is what really matters, and if you're anything like me, you want to know you are doing everything in your power to help your loved one.

I'll break down the exact **Dear Family Framework** for you later on in the book, but first, there's one other important thing I need to touch on.

I'm often asked, "How long does this take?" Here's the thing: the answer depends on a whole bunch of factors.

The reality is you have a loved one with a complex, life-threatening, multi-layered illness that, in some cases, has been untreated for 10, 20, or 30-plus years. And you have a family system that's struggling with fear, hurt, and confusion who has been accommodating, putting up with, cutting off, kicking out, and fighting back with the problem for often the same amount of time. That's decades of behaviors, habits, and patterns that need unraveling.

This is work. At times, it is hard, but let me ask you this: is what you've got going on now hard? Hell yes, it is. Harder than anything. Heartbreaking. Devastating. Maddening. So, do you want to keep doing this kind of hard? Or are you ready to do a different kind of hard that will get you out of this mess, get your voice back, and let you live your own life of peace?

This is work. At times, it is hard, but let me ask you this: is what you've got going on now hard?

So, to answer the question of how long this takes, I've seen it take days for people to be like, "OMG, this makes so much sense." The aha moment, the wake up, can be quick.

For others, it may take longer. The path to recovery is different for everyone, but the principles are the same. Getting the process down and the principles integrated into your life is something you as the person reading this book and standing at your own tipping point can control. Implementing them into your life **takes as long as it takes** depending on how willing you are to let the truth in. It works if you work it.

The good news is it gets easier as you go. Each new shift fuels the next, so step away from the microwave "I need it now" mentality for a minute and read on.

It takes as long as it takes.

You will soon learn I'm a regular person who became an expert at something because I was so passionate about it. I was sickened by how compartmentalized and fractured all the systems involved in recovery are. I witnessed the medical system, the civic system, the addiction treatment system, the insurance system, the family system, and the community at large all working alongside each other but with massive gaps in between. And the person with the addiction who these systems are all trying to help—who has little to no sense of self-worth, weakened resiliency, and a lack of internal resources to hang on through all of these transitions—ends up falling through these gaps, unfortunately, often to their death. I became obsessed with bridging these systems and closing the gaps so people would stop falling through the way I almost did.

My own struggles with alcoholism and drug addiction took me to a very dark place. One where I was face down on a bathroom floor, utterly hating my very essence. One where I did unthinkable things like driving drunk and lying to my children, the people I loved most in the world, over and over and over. One where I deliberately eyed the trees along the highway and wondered how fast I would have to drive into one to end it. One where I became someone I not only didn't recognize but couldn't stand.

One day, my daughter, who was sixteen at the time, came right up close to my face and said, "You disgust me." My sister admitted years later that she had been both afraid *for* me and afraid *of* me.

I was mean and cutting. I wanted everyone to *just leave me alone.*

Turns out, I was (unconsciously and unknowingly) trying to get everyone to hate me as much as I hated myself.

None of us knew what to do. I honestly didn't know what was happening to me for years. I attempted outpatient treatment once only to drink within minutes of leaving the group that was held three times a week for an hour. Months later, I was admitted to a fourteen-day treatment program and hung on to my sobriety with a thin rope for two additional weeks. After receiving a thirty-day chip at an AA meeting, the pressure of what it seemed I needed to do had me driving right to a bar and drinking. The progression of my addiction worsened with every one of these attempted stops and ultimately continued to spiral even further over the next year.

My addiction brought the state police to my apartment door. Sometimes my car was not where I thought I had left it. I'd have multiple unexplained bruises on my arms and back from falling down stairs. It reached a point where I knew I either had to get sober or I was going to die.

So one day, I brought myself to the ER, pleading for help, and I never went home. After a week in detox and a thirty-day residential stay, I lived in a sober house for several months followed by living with a sober roommate for over a year. I was afraid if I left the bubble of sobriety and recovery I had created, I would relapse. I knew I needed to be surrounded by a recovery community if I had any chance of my own recovery lasting, and my family didn't know how to be that community for me.

Family *can* be a part of a recovery community. I ultimately determined family is the key to bridging those gaps in the systems I had experienced firsthand, and the more I witnessed the power of family recovery, the more determined I became to share this discovery widely.

I almost didn't share this family recovery framework. In fact, I almost didn't start Tipping Point Recovery at all because of my own self-doubt. I was not a clinician, and during the time I was contemplating creating Tipping Point Recovery, I thought you had to be a clinician to work in the field of addiction and recovery. It turns out not being a clinician was just the thing I needed to see a solution.

Because I hadn't been formally trained within a specific methodology, I wasn't bound by the standards and expectations of any one system. Showing up simply as a peer with the recent experience of being a struggling addict myself granted me the perspective to see a 30,000-foot view of all the systems, which allowed me to discover the power of leveraging family and ultimately create a model to bridge the gaps.

At this point, you might be feeling hopeful that I'm indicating you can help your loved one. So much of the world tells you that you can't or shouldn't.

You might also be wondering, "What about the others in my family? They don't agree that we can or should help. They have a more logical approach and tell me that my loved one should just stop. They don't believe addiction is an illness or disorder, etc."

I get it. I hear this all the time, and I'll touch on it more later. For now, know this:

It doesn't matter about others in your family. It doesn't matter if others don't think you should or can help.

Recovery for your family can begin with only one person, and it doesn't have to be a family member in the traditional sense either. Any person close to the individual struggling can be the catalyst for change, a catalyst for recovery. We'll show you how to get the others to the table.

Recovery is contagious. You'll see.

So, if you're ready to get started on the path to recover your family, let's get started!

CHAPTER 2
WHO THIS BOOK IS FOR

The framework you are about to learn is the result of my collective experiences on all sides of the addiction table. I myself am a recovering addict and alcoholic. I've been in personal relationships with addicts, and I am a family member. After my own recovery began, I worked as a case manager in a detox facility and rehab center as well as a recovery coach in an emergency room prior to founding Tipping Point Recovery. I have supported hundreds of individuals and families through these programs and services. Viewing from these multiple perspectives—addict, family member, and treatment professional—helped me clearly identify the gaping cracks in the current systems of care.

I didn't fully realize the impact family could have on a loved one's recovery until that job in the emergency room.

It was a two-year position funded by a grant in partnership with the district attorney's office, local police department, emergency room, and an addiction treatment center. I was on call 24/7 as a recovery coach in the emergency room, and I would get called in whenever a person experienced a non-fatal overdose.

A non-fatal overdose is when someone overdoses on heroin/opioids and is given the drug naloxone to reverse the effects. My job was to meet the individual at the emergency room and talk with them about treatment and recovery.

WHAT NALOXONE IS AND WHY YOU SHOULD HAVE IT

Naloxone, often referred to by the brand name Narcan, is a drug that rapidly reverses the effects of an opioid overdose. Naloxone is available as both an injection or nasal spray and is recommended to be given immediately to anyone who shows signs of an opioid overdose. It has no effects on someone who has no opioids in their system.

I recommend all families who have a loved one struggling with substance use disorder get naloxone in some form to have on hand in case of emergency. Clients I have worked with have saved their loved ones' lives by having it.

Narcan nasal spray is available over the counter without a prescription, and other naloxone products may be available to you at a pharmacy without a prescription depending on the state where you live.

Be sure to consult with a medical professional to learn how to properly use naloxone.

To learn more, visit:

https://nida.nih.gov/publications/drugfacts/naloxone

During this two-year period, I was called to the emergency room at least once a day. In those first few months of going into the hospital, I learned the first important lesson:

Addiction is widely misunderstood, even in the medical community. So few people know what is really going on with this disease.

The ER staff worked tirelessly to address the patients' immediate and acute needs—however, it became apparent to me that the complex needs of an individual with substance use disorder cannot be met in the ER. The nurses and doctors clearly cared deeply, but they were operating within a system that isn't set up to take on the nuanced challenges that come with addiction.

Emergency rooms aren't equipped for multi-layered conversations about mental health and willingness. They're focused on triage. And because of how misunderstood addiction is as a whole, the solutions offered in the ER aren't the ones most needed at that time.

During my time as a recovery coach there, the patient navigator would walk into a patient's room, clipboard in hand, to get their consent to speak with me. They would ask, "Do you want help?" Nine out of every ten patients said no and would be discharged.

I was shocked as I watched this happen again and again. I naively believed when I started this job that I would walk into that emergency room and be able to reach everyone, and here I was unable to speak with 99% of them. My heart broke more with each discharge. I had an inkling how the patients felt and what they might be going through. I saw the me I had been at the height of my own addiction, drowning in pain I wouldn't (*or couldn't*) admit I had, not knowing how to stop the compulsion to drink, and incapable of finding my own way out.

I knew those patients didn't mean they didn't want help. I knew they felt trapped, suddenly in the ER when they really wanted to be high. I knew they had racing thoughts running through their minds at the messes they'd have to clean up and that they just wanted out. I also knew they had not chosen this path, and that none of this meant they did not want help!

I followed the doctors and nurses down the halls, telling them this. One day, the chief of physicians asked me to come to doctors' rounds to share some of my personal story. On this day, it occurred to me **they were asking the wrong question**, so I asked them to change it.

They were asking the wrong question.

Instead of asking, "Do you want help?" I suggested they ask, "Would you like to speak to an addict?"

Do you know what happened?

Every single one of the patients said yes!

It was because I was a recovering addict that I was able to engage with these patients when other attempts had failed, and it was because of that same perspective that the patients started opening up to me.

The question I got asked the most?

"Will you talk to my family?"

Maybe that's surprising to hear if your loved one has been hurtful or nasty to you while active in their addiction—we can be *very hurtful and nasty*. I certainly was to my family, but believe me when I say they don't mean it. They really don't. They are not themselves. Trust me!

So, I would meet with their families, and the majority of those families were either confused, scared, hurt, and/or angry. Unbelievably angry. I understood that. I did. I'm not saying their anger wasn't justified, but I also knew being surrounded by anger and fear does not lead to recovery.

The alcoholic/addict is filled with their own anger, shame, guilt, and pain. To be met by that same anger, shame, and pain does not give recovery much of a chance.

What's more—all that anger and hurt? It was almost always directed at the wrong thing.

It's something I see with most of the families that come to work with us. There is naturally so much emotion about the addiction and behaviors it is causing that families are often throwing solutions at the wall in the dark. They're navigating through a thick fog of yuck, pointing out ideas, beliefs, and potential solutions at what they think the problem is without realizing that the thing they are fighting is their loved one while the real enemy—the addiction—goes untouched. In too many cases, it's the addiction that is winning.

Sometimes that fight is in the form of them doing everything for their loved one, trying to single-handedly keep the addiction from spiraling out of control. (Spoiler: this is impossible.)

Sometimes the fight looks more like washing their hands of it, thinking it's their loved one's problem, so why should they have to do anything to fix it?

Sometimes it's them just being flat out done, wanting nothing to do with their loved one at all because they think it's a lost cause.

What became clear to me with the families I met at the hospital was that all this fighting led back to the same problem:

On the one hand, there was an addict who was self-medicating their pain and fear with drugs, and on the other hand was the family who was self-medicating their pain and fear with anger and/or compassion that often resulted in being complicit or accommodating.

Pain and fear plus pain and fear do not equal recovery.

$$(Pain/Fear) + (Pain/Fear) \neq Recovery$$

So, I started a family support and education group. I gathered these families around a conference table in a community health center and taught them about addiction from the perspective of a recovering addict. I listened to them talk about their loved ones. I let them vent their anger. I held space for them to say sometimes terrible things about what a jerk and disgusting human being their loved one was.

Then I told them how I was exactly like that; I was their loved one. I shared stories of what I had done, and I shared some of the terrible things I had said to those I loved.

I told them *why* I had done and said those things.

Most important of all, I told them this:

Your loved one is getting swallowed up.

And *you* are getting swallowed up.

This approach is not working.

What your loved one is doing isn't by choice, and you've gotten caught up in the mix.

You're lost. You can't catch your breath. You don't have peace. You're spiraling.

You've become entangled. Your life is either completely focused on trying to manage your loved one's addiction or recovery, or you're trying to compartmentalize and get them out of your head and just stop thinking about it.

The bottom line is that you've lost a piece, or multiple pieces, of your life just like your addicted loved one has. They're unwell and so are you. Neither of you deserves that, but you're in no shape to help them because sick can't heal sick.

I continued to meet with these families every week for two years. At the end of those two years, I noticed two specific improvements in those who attended:

One, the family members were getting well.

And two, nearly all of their loved ones were on some kind of path in recovery.

I knew then it wasn't a coincidence. One of the moms of the group even walked up to me, handed me her notebook, and said, "I wrote down everything you said." I used her notes from my teachings to help create my first online program, and all the work I've done with families in the years since has proven the same thing over and over again.

Truly, one of the most powerful things you can do for your loved one is to recover yourself. Process your anger, untangle yourself from the chaos, and allow for your voice and your peace to return.

It is my sincere hope that you'll use the teachings in this book to develop the skills and tools you need to break the web of addiction that you've been caught in and feel empowered in your life again. As a result, you'll be creating bandwidth for your loved one to get better, because the same way addiction is contagious, recovery is as well.

This book is for those who are ready to create change, begin to put themselves back together, and get grounded in their own recovery so their loved ones can do the same.

Check-In Assessment

Before we continue with the rest of the book, let's check in on where you're at right now on your own recovery journey.

Rate the following statements on a scale of 0-10—10 meaning "I fully agree" and 0 meaning "I don't agree at all."

Once you've gone through each statement, total up the score and use the answer key to guide your next steps.

Addiction Impact Statement	Score
I understand addiction is a complex disorder and the ways it impacts an individual on physical, mental, emotional, and spiritual levels.	
I understand addiction as a family disorder, that I have become unwell, and in what ways I am not my best self.	
I know what recovery looks like and what my loved one needs to experience recovery.	
I know the stages of recovery and the stages of change.	
I fully believe in my loved one's ability to recover.	
I refrain from taking responsibility and action for my loved one's well-being.	
I am on a clear path of recovery for myself and enjoy a peaceful, balanced, and joyful life.	
I am part of a community where I receive regular support on my recovery journey.	
I feel healthy, energized, and joyful most of the time.	
I live a life aligned with my values.	
Total Score:	

What Your Score Means

Score 0-40

You're Stuck in the Fog

I've got good news and bad news. The bad news is you are caught in the fog addiction wants you to stay in, and therefore, you have no framework for understanding the full scope of what is going on for your loved one and how you're tied into all of it. Without that understanding, it's difficult for you to access what is needed for everyone in your family to achieve lasting peace, health, and recovery.

It's not your fault that you're in the dark.

No one told you the truth before now. The good news is this book is here to change that. I invite you to continue reading with an open mind. Some of what I teach in the following chapters may bring up a complicated mix of feelings if you're hearing it for the first time, but even embracing only some of it will lead to impactful changes for you and your loved one.

Score 41-75

Stronger Understanding Will Go a Long Way Toward Making Changes

If your score landed you here, it means you've started to pull back the curtain on the truth around addiction and recovery, but there are still a few key concepts or principles you either haven't yet explored or that just haven't quite clicked for you.

You likely know and believe addiction is a disease and see some of the ways you have become unwell as a result, but you may still struggle to act on that knowledge or change your behavior and fully embrace recovery for yourself or even believe recovery is possible for you or your loved one.

Taking a few new actions will go a long way in creating the shift you need to go from *knowing* the truth to *experiencing* the truth. Get ready for a whole new way of communicating with your loved one and connecting not only with them but with yourself.

Score 76-100

You're Ready To Tackle Your Own Inner Recovery Work

Your eyes are wide open to what's really going on with addiction both for your loved one and yourself. You get that you can't force your loved one to get better, you know they aren't choosing to continue down this path all on their own, and you know the best way you can help them is to help yourself.

Your biggest hurdle is understanding exactly how to do that.

That's where this book comes in. We'll guide you on how to focus on yourself and walk your own recovery path so you can not only clear the way for your loved one to follow suit and know when and how to offer real help but so you can experience your life fully, openly, and whole-heartedly again, no matter what is going on with your loved one.

KEY CHAPTER TAKEAWAYS

❖ Addiction is as widely misunderstood among the medical community as it is everywhere else. So few people know what is really going on with this disease.

❖ It's common for families to be hurt, mad, sad, and confused toward their loved ones, but because families are not typically part of the solution, they are kept in the dark about what to do and how to help.

❖ Families become unwell as a result of being in proximity to addiction.

❖ The most powerful thing families can do to help their loved ones recover is to recover themselves.

❖ Recovered, empowered, educated, and stronger family systems improve recovery outcomes.

CHAPTER 3
THE 3 TRAPS FAMILIES FALL FOR
(AND HOW TO FREE YOURSELF FROM THEM WITH THIS FRAMEWORK)

Since finding my own recovery, I've worked as a case manager in a detox and rehab facility, as a recovery coach, and as an interventionist. I have been trained and mentored by some of the most established and reputable professionals in the field.

Over the years, I've worked with hundreds of husbands and wives, mothers and fathers, grandparents, siblings, partners, aunts and uncles, cousins, and friends, both individually and in groups, to help them get their loved ones into treatment and onto a path toward lasting change.

All this to say: I've learned a few things about family recovery.

I want to share the three traps I most often see families fall for when trying to help their addicted loved ones. I'm doing this for two reasons:

1. So you can be aware of these traps and avoid falling into them yourself.
2. To show you how complex addiction really is and why it's so important to gain a full understanding of it in order to offer real help.

It may feel as you read through these traps like I'm blaming you for your loved one's situation. That is not at all what I'm doing because none of this is your fault. Let me say that again:

None of this is your fault.

To quote Al-Anon's three C's, "You didn't cause it, you can't control it, and you can't cure it." What I think is missing from this statement is, "But you *can* detach from it. You *can* be a catalyst for change. You *can* recover."

Part of that recovery is identifying ways you may inadvertently be complicit so that you can take steps to stop. These traps are meant to help you gain that awareness.

~❖~

Trap #1: Waiting for Them to "Want" It

It's possible the thing I hate hearing more than anything else when it comes to addiction and recovery is, "They have to want it." Families hear (and say) this *all the time*. That until the person with the addiction wants to get better badly enough, there's nothing anyone else can do to help them. That their willingness is the key.

This has not been my experience, and this thinking is a trap that keeps people sick.

Stick with me here.

Thinking they have to "want" it is why so often when families first meet with me, they tell me things like, "She's already tried treatment, and it didn't work. She just isn't ready yet or doesn't want to get better," or they'll ask, "Well, what if he isn't willing to go to treatment? What if he doesn't want to quit?"

They *do* want it. Your loved one does want to get better. A part of them does. It's their addiction that doesn't, and their addiction is currently calling the shots, so it's the addiction's resistance that you see.

Addiction is treatment resistant.

Another thing to keep in mind is it's not only about what your loved one wants or is willing to do. It's about what they *need*, and what you want and need matters too. Your loved one may not want treatment, but it doesn't change the fact that they need it. What I want families to know is this: you do not have to wait for all of the wheels to fall off before creating change. You do not have to wait for them to feel ready for change before you begin to change.

Addiction is a disease where, far too often, we wait for it to get worse before it gets treated. What's crucial to understand about addiction is most people struggling aren't capable of "wanting" to get better until they *start* to get better.

Read that again.

It's the deadliest catch-22 I know.

What do I mean by that?

Imagine sitting down at a restaurant. The waiter hands you the menu and asks you what you want, and when you look at the options, they're all things you've never heard of before. They might as well be written in a different language; that's how foreign these foods are to you. So how are you supposed to pick what you want? How can you crave something when you have no idea what it looks like, smells like, or tastes like?

That's what "wanting" recovery is like for someone in active addiction. They can't even imagine it, never mind want it. In their minds, the idea of something else, of something better, seems so obscure, so far-fetched, and they don't even believe it's possible.

What's more, people active in their addiction don't really like themselves enough to want more for themselves. Most don't have the internal resources to hold any amount of "want" long enough to do what's necessary.

Now, imagine the waiter brings out an appetizer for the table, a little sample to start off your meal. You try it, uncertain at first, but it actually tastes pretty good, different from anything you've eaten in a long time. It's a little unfamiliar, but the longer the taste lingers in your mouth, the more of it you want.

That's what treatment does for someone with substance use disorder. It gives them a taste of what life could be like without the drugs or alcohol they've become addicted to, and without that taste, they can't imagine that a better life is even possible or attainable. They can't imagine what "better" looks like or that "better" even exists. They can't imagine that they can do what it takes or that they deserve it. It doesn't mean they want to keep living the way they are now. In fact, I can guarantee you they don't, but their addiction is keeping them from seeing any other way.

Take one of the young men whose family I worked with to help him get sober. His mom had used Section 35 on him—Section 35 being a Massachusetts law that allows someone with substance use disorder to be civilly committed and treated involuntarily—and he was *furious* about it. He hadn't "wanted" the help. He'd hated his mom for doing it to him and stayed angry with her for months, even close to a year. Years later after getting sober and achieving recovery, he shared with our member community that it was getting Sectioned that allowed him to begin to see a glimpse of what being sober might be like and that getting sober might be possible for him. He said it made him realize he might even like it.

Now, is willingness important? Of course. You can't force someone to stop drinking or doing drugs. Section 35 may not be the long-term solution. You can't do someone else's recovery for them. If you're reading this book, you've probably already tried to do just that, so I don't need to tell you how poorly that turns out.

But someone doesn't have to "want" it to begin to be willing. In fact, **treatment is designed for those who don't want it**, and each attempt, each bit of treatment, each sober period, gets stacked on top of the last to create more want.

Willingness comes and goes. You know this—you've prob-ably seen those (sometimes fleeting) moments when the window of willingness opens briefly only to slam shut min-utes later. Those moments when someone shows an inkling of being sick and tired of being sick and tired. Those are the parts of your loved one surfacing that *do* want it. They are in there. It's those moments that you, as their loved one, can be available for by being plugged into your own recovery so you have the resources available to orient your loved one on their own path.

Check-In Assessment

Before we continue with the rest of the book, let's check in on where you're at right now with waiting for your loved one to want it.

Rate the following statements on a scale of 0-10—10 meaning "I fully agree" and 0 meaning "I don't agree at all."

Once you've gone through each statement, total up the score and use the answer key to guide your next steps.

Check-In Assessment	Score
I believe most people who are struggling with substance use disorder do want recovery.	
I understand that most people in active addiction lack care about themselves enough to recover for themselves.	
I understand that even when someone relapses after treatment, it doesn't mean treatment didn't work.	
I know that most in active addiction lack the internal resources necessary to "want" to recover.	
I recognize the windows of willingness my loved one shows and understand them to be the part of my loved one that wants to recover.	
Total Score:	

What Your Score Means

Score 0-25

You're Waiting for Them to Want It (and Letting Addiction Lead the Way)

If your score landed here, you're very likely having trouble accepting addiction as a disease or disorder. It makes sense you're having this struggle because addiction is largely not viewed this way by society or portrayed this way in mainstream media.

The most powerful thing you can do right now to help your loved one is to understand the truth of what's really going on with addiction. Luckily, that's exactly what we dive into further on in this book. Continue reading, and keep an open mind to a new way of thinking about addiction.

Score 26-39

A Few Small Changes Will Help You Close the Gap

In theory, you understand addiction is not a choice, but in the day-to-day reality, your emotions, fear, and exasperation pull you to react as though it *is* a choice. There's a gap between what you're learning and how you're showing up.

The way to close this gap is to deepen your understanding of addiction so this new knowledge becomes more fully integrated into your responses. Through practicing the new ways of thinking and communicating laid out in this book, you will be better prepared to respond in an effective way when those windows of willingness open rather than scrambling in the chaos.

Score 40-50

You're Ready for a Deep Dive into the Framework

You accept that addiction isn't a choice, and your responses are grounded in recovery. Your greatest challenge is you need guidance for what to do as this cunning and baffling disease progresses.

That's where the **Dear Family Framework** comes in. We'll give you specific tools to spot the symptoms of addiction, find your own lane, and make recovery-oriented decisions so that you are equipped to do everything you can to offer the best chance of success for your loved one.

Trap #2: Thinking There's Nothing You Can Do

When I was deep in my alcoholism and driving drunk one evening, my sister went to an anonymous family support meeting in search of guidance for what she could do to help me in that moment. A group of very kind women were there, knitting in a circle, and when my sister turned up panicked about me driving drunk and was desperate to stop me, one of the women simply smiled and said, "Turn it over to God, dear."

Now in fairness, this group's purpose was to provide family support amidst the effects of living with a family member, friend, or relative with addiction. It was not education or guidance like our programs. They gave assistance that fit the support-based lens of their program, but it's an example of what families are told all throughout the world, even in the recovery world and by some treatment centers: that there's nothing they can do for their loved ones.

This is just not true.

It ties back to this idea that you can't force someone to recover, which is true, but it overlooks the fact that there are a *huge* number of things families can do to increase their loved ones' chances of recovery.

You can

1. learn about addiction and what is really going on (this is a key part of our framework that we'll be diving into in a little bit);

2. learn the ways you may be inadvertently acting as a resource for the addiction and how to stop;

3. learn how to become a resource for recovery instead (also more on this later);

4. notice your own patterns that you've become stuck in that are no longer serving you;

5. take inventory of what addiction is currently costing you—financially, emotionally, physically, and spiritually;

6. start caring more about your own well-being;

7. hold on to the belief (or come to find it) that your loved one can recover; and

8. find a new strength through community—FIND YOUR PEOPLE.

This list is just a start. There are countless more things you can do to orient your loved one toward recovery. The key to it all is really this: do for yourself what you want for them.

If you want them to start taking accountability for their actions, make sure you are accounting for yours. If you want them to be honest about how they are doing, be honest about how you are doing. If you want them to take better care of themselves, start prioritizing your own self-care. Even something as specific as if you want them to go to a meeting, get to your own (more on this later).

I know it feels counterintuitive, but I promise you this is what makes the difference. It's cause and effect in action. When you create change, the people around you will change.

Now, while there are lots of things you *can* do to help your loved one, there are also lots of things you want to be sure *not* to do, things that inadvertently contribute to the problem and may even be harmful. Have you heard the phrase, "Doing nothing is doing something?" In this case, you may *think* you're doing nothing when you may actually be feeding into the problem without realizing it.

If you get nothing else from this book, I at least want to make sure that you learn how to stop doing anything that might be contributing to the problem. Things like

1. letting your loved one's addiction call the shots and following their lead;

2. reacting from fear or urgency rather than responding with practical, helpful strategies and boundaries;

3. rushing to make decisions without giving yourself the time and space to determine if it will help or harm;

4. not getting a professional perspective before acting; and

5. financially supporting your loved one's addiction instead of treatment.

These may require professional guidance and support to handle most effectively. In fact, I strongly recommend getting professional guidance as these changes are difficult and nuanced. We'll discuss in later chapters some tools to help, but if you'd like the guidance and support of our expert team, schedule a call with us here: https://tippingpointrecovery.as.me/connection-call.

Of the items listed above, financial support is also probably the hardest one for families to come to terms with. Whenever I first suggest this to the families I work with, especially parents, they usually come back with questions.

"What if I just buy her groceries?"

"How will he get to work if I don't pay for his car?"

"But if I stop paying their rent, where will they live?"

I get it. I do. Of course you want to make sure your loved one has what they need to get by. My parents did, too. Clouded by my addicted thinking, I convinced my parents that I needed help when I was drinking heavily and hiding it. I told them I didn't have enough money, so they helped pay my rent. By doing so, that meant I could take the money I would have had to spend on rent and use it to buy more wine.

I was sick.

Same with groceries. If my parents paid for them, it freed up my dollars to spend on booze, all while allowing me to be comfortable in my addiction with a full stomach and a roof over my head.

It may not feel like enabling because you're not buying the drugs or booze for your loved one, but by paying for the things they would otherwise have to pay for themselves, you are acting as a resource for the addiction by freeing up their own money for substances, and *that* is contributing to the problem.

So yes, there is a lot that you can do to orient your loved one toward recovery, but just as important, there's a lot that you *don't* want to do that could potentially contribute to your loved one's addiction cycle. Understanding what those things are is the first step you can take to changing your own behavior.

Go ahead and take a moment to check in with yourself.

Check-In Assessment

Before we continue with the rest of the book, let's check in on where you're at right now with thinking there's nothing you can do.

Rate the following statements on a scale of 0-10—10 meaning "I fully agree" and 0 meaning "I don't agree at all."

Once you've gone through each statement, total up the score and use the answer key to guide your next steps.

Check-In Assessment	Score
I know when it comes to addiction that my actions have an impact whether they are helpful or not.	
I believe there are actions I can take that will have a positive impact on my loved one's chances at lasting recovery.	
I carefully assess each of my actions to determine whether it may be contributing to the problem.	
I regularly hold myself to the same standards I seek from my loved one.	
I understand the difference between being a resource for addiction versus a resource for recovery and am confident in differentiating the two in my day-to-day life.	
Total Score:	

What Your Score Means

Score 0-25

Time for a Whole New Perspective

If you scored in this range, it's possible that before reading this chapter you'd not heard this before, but there *is* something you can do to help your loved one. If you are just hearing it for the first time, you may be a bit skeptical that it's true. After all, I'm asking you to shift into a new perspective. Your task right now is to consider believing that it is true.

I know it's true because I see families making a difference for their loved ones every day, and I wrote this book so you could see it too. The entire **Dear Family Framework** was developed to empower families with the knowledge and tools needed to give their loved ones the best chance of success, and it was developed through working with families and their loved ones directly. The firmer you become in your belief of what you can do and the ways you are not powerless in this situation, the better equipped you will be to wield that power for recovery.

Just like your loved one doesn't have to fully accept they are an alcoholic or addict in order to begin to consider the idea, you don't need to fully believe in this perspective in order to give it a try. Even if you only pick out one new thing to do from this book, that thing is one step in a new direction. There isn't anything that can't be accomplished one step at a time. Choose the step that feels manageable for you, and remember, help is available for you whenever you need it, whether from our team or from one of the other supports we mention throughout the book.

Score 26-39

Onboard but Ungrounded

You fully believe there are things you can do to help your loved one. In fact, you are likely relieved to hear it. You may have even been trying different things already, jumping in with both feet to whatever you heard about that might help.

The issue you are likely facing is that all the things you are trying are still focused on your loved one, leaving you scattered in a thousand different directions trying to hold the pieces together.

What you need is to get grounded back to yourself so the action you take can come from a solid, clear-headed space. This means untangling yourself from your loved one and getting clear on what's yours versus what's theirs and what you can control versus what you can't. We have a whole section on this later on in the framework to help you get started. It's from this grounded place that you'll be better able to determine what action will be most beneficial in the long run.

Score 40-50

Connection Is Key

With a score this high, you've likely already done a fair amount of work on building up a recovery community for yourself, paying attention to your own actions, and distancing yourself from the addiction.

What many families struggle with at this stage is how to connect with their loved ones in meaningful ways. After all, your loved one and their addiction are two separate things, but it can be difficult to know how to connect with one while turning the other way.

It is absolutely possible for you to still connect with your loved one. (It's one of the most powerful results of the **Dear Family Framework**.) Learning to spot the symptoms of addiction and recognize recovery will go a long way in helping you bridge this gap, along with learning new ways to communicate with your loved one, which we touch on later in the framework.

Trap #3: Caring About Their Feelings (and your own) More Than Their (and your) Recovery

I had a client years ago who went back and forth for months about whether or not to do an intervention for her husband who was an alcoholic. The thing holding her back was how the process reminded her of when her family intervened on her mother with Alzheimer's, who ended up dying in rehab.

When I read that text message from her, what I heard was her fear preventing her from helping both herself and her husband: *"I don't think I could handle my husband dying in rehab, so therefore, I'm not going to do anything."*

Or another translation: *"I'm going to accept the pain and chaos I'm currently in, as it is potentially more tolerable than the unknown of change."*

Another time, a woman came to me because her sister was drinking heavily. I asked her about the possibility of raising the issue with her sister, to which she said, "Oh no. I can't talk with her about it. She'll never speak to me again."

This happens frequently with families I meet. They feel afraid to address things with their loved ones regarding their substance use because they are worried their loved ones will be mad at them or that something worse will happen as a result.

While this fear makes sense, at the core of this, we are putting our own feelings—most specifically our fear—ahead of someone's potential recovery and well-being.

We're so afraid to do the thing we know they need that we don't do anything.

I know this may sound harsh, but it's one of the hard truths I teach. I'd rather hear the hard truth than stay in the illusion that I'm helping.

I get it. I do. This was me years ago with my own loved one. This *is* scary. It is terrifying.

But, the truth is addiction is progressive and will only get worse. You can become stronger than your fear.

Might your loved one be angry with you for helping them in the way they need to be helped rather than in the way they (and their addiction) want? That is very likely. Can you see yourself coming to a place where them being mad is outweighed by the desire to offer them the help they really need?

Your loved one does not need you to coddle them. To coddle them while they're active in their addiction is to coddle their addiction. They do not need you to make their life comfortable while they actively harm themselves.

What we see again and again, with the loved ones of the families we work with and the people in recovery who join us as guest speakers in our programs, is that one of the things that makes the greatest difference in their success is for you as their loved one to put their recovery (and your own wellness) as the number-one priority in your relationship with them. And that will probably mean facing your own fear in the process.

It's hard, and it's scary, but remember—there is a part of your loved one that wants to get better, and that part of them won't hate you for hurting their feelings for the sake of their recovery. That part will thank you for it once they are better. It's the addiction that is angry—not your loved one.

Also remember that fear is just another tool of addiction.

Don't let your fear overrule your courage to create change.

Don't let the addiction bully you into losing someone you love.

When you prioritize their recovery over their feelings, there's a much higher chance they'll find their long-term recovery path. I know because I see it every day.

Check-In Assessment

Before we continue with the rest of the book, let's check in on where you're at right now with caring about your own feelings over your loved one's recovery.

Rate the following statements on a scale of 0-10—10 meaning "I fully agree" and 0 meaning "I don't agree at all."

Once you've gone through each statement, total up the score and use the answer key to guide your next steps.

Check-In Assessment	Score
I regularly confront and accept my own fears in order to fully embrace the recovery process.	
I engage with my loved one in ways that I know are helpful for their recovery despite sometimes being uncomfortable for me.	
I accept that my loved one may be angry with me at times as I learn to support only their recovery.	
I sometimes sacrifice my own comfort to try a new way of doing things, even though it scares me.	
I know that when my loved one lashes out, it is their addiction that's angry with me, not the part of my loved one that wants to recover.	
I accept that the relationship I have with my loved one might change as I start to do things differently. I'm okay with this if it means they find recovery.	
Total Score:	

Score 0-20

You're Trying to Carry It All

Right now, there's a good chance you think it's all on your shoulders—your loved one's well-being, their recovery, and their emotional state. Their problems are your problems; their pain is your pain. You may be so entangled that it's got you paralyzed, trapped in absolute fear that if you make the wrong choice, everything will collapse.

I'm here to tell you it's not all on your shoulders. Whether your loved one recovers is not up to you. Whether you do the things within your power to give them the best chance for recovery is.

Learning the difference between those two things is a great place to start. In the **Dear Family Framework,** we call it Finding Your Lane, and we'll dive into that in detail later on. For now, just know that none of what you are carrying is a weight you have to keep carrying alone. Once you set down what isn't yours and gain confidence in managing what is, it won't be a weight that holds you down any longer.

Score 21-40

Feed What Makes You Strong

You have started to gain an understanding of the ways you may have put your loved one's feelings ahead of their recovery in the past, but your struggle now is how to let your loved one have their own experience and still be okay, especially when your loved one's experience creates discomfort for them.

Look, there's a reason I call the families I work with the Brave Ones. Putting your loved one's recovery ahead of their feelings takes monumental courage and an incredible amount of strength. It takes practice to learn how to separate your reaction to what they're doing from how it makes you feel, to keep your emotions in your own lane for you to process and leave their stuff in their lane for them to deal with.

This is where working a recovery program within a community comes in. There is no better way to build the strength you need than within a container of others doing the same. It's why community is one of the three key components of the **Dear Family Framework**. We'll dive into those in the next chapter, so keep reading.

Score 41-60

Put the Tools in Place

You're likely solid enough in your own recovery that you've mostly unplugged from the chaos of your loved one's addiction and are able to put their recovery first…at least, when you know how. Chances are, it's not always clear which step you should take to best support recovery or which action would be most useful in orienting your loved one toward a new path.

Having specific systems in place, like our Decision-Making Blueprint that's part of our **Dear Family Framework**, will help you determine which actions most align with your intentions and will allow you to be consistent in your own recovery. The more you practice putting these tools into place, ideally with the guidance of a professional, the more powerful a resource for recovery you will become.

KEY CHAPTER TAKEAWAYS

❖ **Trap #1: Waiting for Them to "Want" It.** Your loved one may not want treatment, but that doesn't change the fact that they need it. Most people struggling aren't capable of "wanting" to get better until they start to get better. The good news is that treatment is designed for those who don't want it, and since willingness comes and goes, you can be plugged into your own recovery and have the resources available to orient your loved one on their own path.

❖ **Trap #2: Thinking There's Nothing You Can Do.** There are a lot of actions you can take that will orient your loved one toward recovery, and there are just as many actions you want to be certain you *aren't* taking that inadvertently perpetuate the addiction. Professional guidance is recommended for determining which is which as so much about this is nuanced.

❖ **Trap #3: Caring About Their Feelings (and your own) More Than Their (and your) Recovery.** It can be scary to do the things that your loved one needs, especially when those things make your loved one angry at you. As family members, we're often so afraid to do the thing we know our loved ones need that we don't do anything, but the number one thing our loved ones need from us is to put their recovery before all else. And that will probably mean having to face your own fears in the process.

CHAPTER 4
THE KEYS TO UNLOCKING A FAMILY RECOVERY FRAMEWORK

For decades, the only widespread resource for families of someone with substance use disorder was anonymous family support groups. These groups have a model that works for some. Many of the families that come to Tipping Point Recovery who have been or are a part of anonymous family support groups feel quickly supported, are immediately relieved by the addition of our tools and resources, and are eager to embrace this new approach.

While working in the ER, I referred hundreds of people to these types of groups, and I didn't just refer them—I pushed, begged, even. I sold these groups to families the same way

I sold treatment to their loved ones, and literally almost no one actually went and stuck it out.

Some went to one or two meetings and never went back. It's pretty common to hear, and that's the case for many families I work with. I couldn't help but wonder why.

Ultimately, people want answers. They want strategies. They want to make sense of what is happening to their loved one. They want to help. They want to know what they can do. They want to know what they might be doing that's unhelpful.

What I have observed through my years of work, specifically with families, is that anonymous family support groups alone aren't enough, and it's because they only provide one of the three components that are crucial to an effective family recovery framework.

Let's break down what these components are and why all three are needed to turn and leverage families to be catalysts for change.

~ ❖ ~

Component #1: Community

Community is where anonymous family support groups shine (that is, if you keep going!). When I mentioned how the families coming to Tipping Point Recovery are often more grounded from being in such groups, it's because they had community and an acceptance that their loved ones' addictions were not their fault. You can walk into a meeting and find dozens of people who understand what you're going through as a family member or close friend of an addict, and that's a powerful thing.

You may have heard the phrase, "No one recovers alone." It's really true. Recovery happens in a community. It might be the most important of our components for that reason alone, and it's not something most people really understand until they experience it.

Take me for example. I didn't go to my first AA meeting looking for peers or to be supported by those around me; I was miserable and totally self-absorbed in my own pain. But once I was there, I realized the people around me were filling me up because I couldn't fill myself up.

My pain is what got me there, but the community is what *kept* me there. The very same is true for families.

New families don't come to us saying, "I really need community. I really need to be around others."

They come saying, "I don't want to do this anymore. My loved one won't change. I don't know what else to do." It's after months in our program and 24/7 access to each other in our private online forum that the community they've found is the thing they value above all.

So, whether it's an anonymous family support group, our own Family Recovery Membership, or our weekly Double Circle Meeting, find your community. Because no matter your recovery journey, none of us do it alone.

WHAT IS A DOUBLE CIRCLE MEETING?

Addiction is messy, scary, and maddening—for everyone. Double Circle Meeting is a chance for _all_ those impacted by addiction to come together in a community to heal on mirrored paths—both those in recovery from drugs and alcohol and those who identify as family and friends.

This is a recovery meeting where you will experience the following:

• Hear from people who've been right where you are.

- Listen to another perspective (the addict's perspective if you're a loved one and vice versa).

- Experience the power of community support and connection.

- Restore peace, ease, and joy in your life.

Meetings are held every week over Zoom. You can register to join us at https://www.tippingpointrecovery.com/recovery-meeting/.

Component #2: Education

I was in rehab the first time I learned addiction is a brain disorder. It was in the halls of AA that I heard it referred to as a thinking problem, not a drinking problem; a *thinking* problem.

It made so much sense to me when I heard it that way, and I remember thinking to myself, *why doesn't everyone know this?* Why was this information kept hidden away in church basements for only those in recovery to learn? Why was nobody out there telling my family this?

I wanted my family to hear it. I wanted them to know that it hadn't been my choice to end up where I did, to do the things I had done, or to put them through the pain I had caused. I wanted them to understand how trapped I had felt, how powerless against myself I had been, and that it wasn't just me being weak. I wasn't just a piece of shit after all. For so long, I had felt nothing but shame, but learning this information made me feel like maybe I didn't have to.

Education is empowering in that way. For those in recovery, it empowers us to better understand ourselves and our disease so we can better navigate it. What's currently overlooked is that the same education can help our families understand us just as much, and in doing so, can make recovery more accessible and a more healing process for everyone involved.

Something we'll touch on as we dive into the framework later on—and that is at the center of all our family programs—is how when it comes to addiction, a family's path often mirrors the path of their loved one who is struggling. Family members might not be addicted to substances, but they're caught in their own compulsive loop of harmful patterns just like their loved ones. The same level of self-reflection and understanding is needed to break the cycle (more on this in Chapter 7).

This means learning what is really going on with addiction because it's not what most people think.

It means knowing that addiction is an illness and how it works.

It means recognizing addiction as a *family* disease and knowing the ways it wraps families up in its chaos.

It means understanding what recovery looks like so you can respond in a way that offers real help just like any other disease.

The beauty of gaining this education is it accomplishes two things at once: it helps you to help your loved one, and it helps you to help yourself.

———

Everything we teach you that is for your own best interest also benefits your loved one, and everything we teach you that is for the good of your loved one also benefits you.

———

It is from the place of understanding that you hold the most power to affect change.

Component #3: Tools & Resources

If you've ever tried out a new skill, you're aware that *knowing* what to do and actually *doing* it are two very different things.

I mean, sure, *in theory* I know how to bake a cake. Mix all the ingredients together, pour it into a pan, and pop it in the oven until it's done. Yet if you locked me in a kitchen with all the ingredients set out in front of me and told me to bake a cake on my own, I'd be lost.

How much flour do I need? Am I supposed to use both baking powder *and* baking soda? Is there even a difference? Which ingredients do I mix together first? How long should I bake it for?

For me to have any chance at success, I need a recipe.

That's what the tools and resources of this framework are: a guide to refer back to that makes it much easier to put new skills to practice, with actual steps you can take right away and examples of what you can say to get a different response. A recovery recipe, if you will.

It's the combination of these tools and resources along with education and community that is the key to this framework's success. You need all three for effective change.

We see people who have been part of anonymous family support groups for many years, and while they're more grounded with better self-care and a sense of what is theirs to work on, they often don't understand healthy and effective ways to help their loved ones. They don't know there are numerous methods of intervening available to them. They lack education and tools. They are often literally just watching their loved ones spiral. That isn't a solution.

Some of our clients have attended these groups for years and appreciate them greatly, but they came to us because their loved ones weren't getting better. They wanted to know if there was something else they could do, a way to take care of themselves *and* help their loved ones at the same time.

There is.

It's what we do.

In our programs, we guide you with what to do *and* we show you how to do it. We hold you within the container of our programs while you do it, providing lectures, courses, retreats, and workbook materials to allow you to go even deeper. We tell you when you need to let go, then show you *how* to let go. We teach you what a boundary is, and then we show you how to set one and how to hold it when it gets pushed. We give you the opportunity to watch others do it too. We talk about what it feels like to do it so you can process your emotions out loud.

You get to bring all of yourself into this framework, and in doing so, you unlock the possibility for lasting recovery for your whole family.

Check-In Assessment

Before we continue with the rest of the book, let's check in on where you're at currently with having these components in your toolkit.

Rate the following statements on a scale of 0-10—10 meaning "I fully agree" and 0 meaning "I don't agree at all."

Once you've gone through each statement, total up the score and use the answer key to guide your next steps.

Check-In Assessment	Score
I have a strong community of other families going through a similar situation with their loved ones who are also embarking on a recovery journey.	
I have found a fellowship that resonates with me, and I regularly attend meetings.	
I understand what is really going on with addiction and what it means that addiction is a family disease.	
I understand what recovery looks like and what it takes to recover from substance use disorder.	
I know where to find reliable resources to learn more about addiction and recovery.	
I have access to specific tools to help me practice recovery skills, such as setting healthy boundaries (and maintaining them) and communicating in a recovery-oriented way.	
I have access to professional guidance to ask questions and get answers on the best steps to take to help my loved one.	
Total Score:	

Score 0-28

You Don't Have to Keep Doing This Alone

Right now, you're struggling. Trying to navigate any of this alone is beyond overwhelming. Even treatment professionals still find it confusing at times.

By arming yourself with these three components, you'll no longer have to keep trying to figure everything out on your own. There are answers out there to your questions. There are people who have been where you are. There are resources listed in this book that can get you started on exploring these components for yourself.

Score 29-50

Focusing on Additional Components Will Strengthen What You've Got

You've started building up your recovery arsenal, but one or two of your components are still lacking. Maybe you've been attending a fellowship and your community is strong but you lack specific tools and resources to take action. Or maybe you've had private coaching or have read up on addiction but you've largely done it in isolation. You need that community of others who know exactly what you're going through to help hold you up.

Having all three components will allow you to access a whole new level of recovery. Pay attention as you read on to which parts of the **Dear Family Framework** feel the least familiar to you (or maybe the most uncomfortable). Chances are, those are the parts you could benefit most from focusing on.

Score 51-70

Work Your Program

You've got a solid recovery program in place for yourself. Amazing!

It's important to remember that recovery is a forever journey. These components aren't something you master once and never need again. They shift and grow alongside you, depending on your situation and needs. By continuing to put the **Dear Family Framework** into practice, you will nurture and strengthen these components so they are ready at hand when something comes up in the future.

KEY CHAPTER TAKEAWAYS

❖ There are three key components to a successful Family Recovery Framework. It takes all three to make a lasting impact for both you and your loved one.

❖ **Component #1: Community.** No one recovers alone, and having a community to ground you and fill you up makes all the difference.

❖ **Component #2: Education.** It's only by understanding the truth of the problem that you can offer a real solution.

❖ **Component #3: Tools & Resources.** Knowing what to do and actually doing it are two very different things. Having tools on hand to pull out as needed makes it much easier to put new skills into practice.

CHAPTER 5
FAQS AND FMES

Things have largely been done the same way for years and years when it comes to addiction recovery:

❖ Recovery meetings held in church basements, hidden away from the public.

❖ Discussions of addiction largely avoided all together, everything about it kept under the rug, leaving only stigma and misinformation to dominate our perceptions.

❖ All the responsibility landing on the struggling individuals' shoulders to stumble their way through a confusing and convoluted process of finding treatment and deciding what to do next—all while dealing with a hijacked brain, mountains of shame, and an obsession to drink or drug that's nearly impossible to overcome on their own.

The systems are compartmentalized. All the different industries are trying their best to make a difference, but they are working in isolation from each other, so the person trying to navigate their way all too often slips out or falls through the gaping holes spanning each step. Meanwhile, aren't we all complicit in the problem if we aren't in the solution? Too many of us put our heads in the sand, perhaps not because we don't want to do something different but because we don't know what to do or how to do it. We are tired!

The CEO of a treatment center told me once that the problems his father faced as a treatment provider fifty years ago are the exact same ones he faces today. What we are doing isn't working. In fact, the problem has gotten so much worse. It continues to get worse, and if we want that to change, then we need to widen the lens of how we approach addiction treatment.

What we are doing isn't working. We need to widen the lens of how we approach addiction treatment.

That's what this framework is all about, bridging the gaps between those compartmentalized parts of the system and widening the lens to address more than just the person with substance use disorder, because we know now that addiction doesn't exist in a vacuum. This framework is a paradigm shift.

Nothing changes if nothing changes.

But, like all change, the **Dear Family Framework** sees a fair share of resistance.

Treatment centers and recovery professionals don't really have the bandwidth to bring families into the fold. When I ask fellow interventionists if they continue to meet with families after their loved ones agree to go to treatment, it's common that I get a confused look followed by, "No, they just want to go back to their lives."

And when it comes to the families themselves, willingness also tends to come in stages. When their loved ones are spiraling hard and "the foot is on the throat" as my colleague and mentor Mike Wilson says, a family's willingness is usually high. They're desperate to try anything. It's when things calm down just a little and the foot on the throat eases up that willingness often wanes. Without the high stress of a crisis, our sadness, fear, confusion, and hurt tend to seep in and prevent us from seeing things clearly and having the courage to navigate a new way. Willingness is often overshadowed by fear, doubt, and guilt, and that resistance sounds a lot like this:

"I want to do this, but my husband doesn't think it will work."

"I don't live near my loved one, so it won't make a difference."

"It's his problem, not mine. I shouldn't be the one doing the work."

"She hasn't had a drink in three days, so she's already doing better. I don't need this."

"They've already gone to treatment a bunch of times; it just doesn't work for them. There's no point in trying again."

"My loved one isn't interested in my help."

"It just feels like too much."

"It's not really *that* bad."

"You just don't understand."

I hear variations of these all the time from families. So often that I've started referring to them as "FMEs."

Frequently Made Excuses.

That's all they are—excuses. All strikingly similar to the excuses addicts make themselves when resisting change:

"It's not my fault."

"It's not going to make a difference."

"I don't have a problem."

"I have it under control."

"Treatment doesn't work for me."

"I don't need help."

"It's not that bad."

"I don't have time for this."

Sound familiar?

These excuses are all about shifting the focus away from yourself. For an addict, that's the addiction's goal because addiction thrives in the dark. It doesn't want to be looked at. It wants everyone to keep doing the same things over and over so it can slip through all the cracks left behind and continue to grow and thrive.

For families, it's usually about avoiding looking at something uncomfortable, something that you don't want to acknowledge because you don't know what the solution is or have fear around making a change. It's sometimes easier to avoid it altogether, to pretend like it's not your responsibility because you're not the one with the problem.

But, the problem of addiction is bigger than one person, and if we're going to make real progress in solving it, we need to turn the finger from pointing at others to looking within.

We need to ask ourselves, "What can I do?" and "What can I change?" Even if we don't feel we are responsible. Even if we don't feel it will make a difference.

What can I do right now?

"Okay, so my husband doesn't think it will work, but what can *I* do on my own to make a change?"

"No, I don't live near my loved one, but her addiction still impacts me, right? So, what can *I* do to make a change in my own life to give her addiction a little less power over me (which means a little less power overall)?"

"It's his problem, not mine. So then, what's *my* problem? I definitely have one, so what can I do to improve that?"

Once this shift happens, it's powerful to witness. Treatment centers that hire us to educate and support their clients' families experience dramatically reduced ACAs (clients leaving against clinician advice). Interventionists working with families who are enrolled in our programs note how different the experience is. Families feel empowered instead of left in the dark.

We can all ask ourselves whether we are complicit in maintaining the status quo that continues to fail the hundreds of thousands of people whose lives are lost each year or whether we want to do something different. The choice is ours either way.

You can choose to read this book and decide not to do any of what I suggest. That is a choice. You can choose to try what we suggest and then walk away when it gets uncomfortable. That is also a choice.

You are always at choice.

Most of us forget that everything we do (and don't do) is a choice. There's power in remembering this. There's even more power in stepping back to really look at our choices and understand why we made them in the first place, to be intentional about whether we want to make the same choices again, and to get curious about the root of our reasons and motivations, whatever the action may be.

If you read this book and decide not to do any of what I suggest, ask yourself, "*Why?*" Is it because you don't think it will work, or is there something else beneath the doubt? Is there something that feels like to try anything new is to step off a ledge without a net and clinging to the familiar feels safer?

If you choose to give our methods a try and then walk away when it gets uncomfortable, ask again, "*Why?*" Is it because you tend to assume (as we all do) that uncomfortable things are bad? Is that always true?

And what was behind the choice to give it a try in the first place? Was it your love for your loved one? For yourself? Something else? Does that reason still hold true?

Only you can ultimately say what your reasons are, just like only you can decide if those reasons are ones you want to hold on to. Understanding our choices in this way can help us stick to them when things get tough, and it can help us change course when our choices are no longer serving us.

Making a choice, whatever it is, is your right.

But know that your choice to walk away is as much a problem for you as your loved one's addiction is for them, so take a moment to think about what you wish they would do, and then join me in the next chapter to dive into this recovery framework together.

KEY CHAPTER TAKEAWAYS

❖ Addiction treatment and recovery systems have largely remained the same over the years. It's time for a paradigm shift in how things are done. This framework does just that by bridging the gaps in the compartmentalized addiction treatment system.

❖ FMEs are used to deflect from the discomfort of facing this complex and painful problem.

❖ If we want the system to change, we are all invited to take our heads out of the sand and point the finger inward. We have to ask ourselves, "What can I do?"

PART
02
THE FRAMEWORK

CHAPTER 6
IT'S NOT ABOUT THE DRUGS AND ALCOHOL

I feel emotion coming up as I write this chapter, and it's because I can't express enough how frustrated I am at the huge gap between what we now know about addiction's impact on the brain and the expectations we place on people with substance use disorder to do things their illness prevents them from being able to do.

Whether you believe addiction is a disease, an illness, or a disorder, we can all agree addiction is complex, progressive, and chronic.

It has symptoms and treatments just like any other disease, but largely because of the way its particular symptoms present, a combination of stigma and unrealistic expectations have developed around addiction that are totally counterproductive.

We expect the person with the illness that manifests as a thinking problem, a coping problem, a lack of willingness, and a detachment from self, who often has little if any internal motivation to create needed change, to be the one driving the bus. It's like expecting someone who has lost their vision to just look at the map and follow it home. Ridiculous, right? It treats addiction like a character flaw and presents the solution as a matter of willpower all while ignoring what the real problem actually is.

Your loved one's root problem is not the drugs, alcohol, sex, porn, shopping, food, or whatever it is they are addicted to. Your loved one's root problem is that they are using this thing, this substance, to try to solve something going on inside of them. Their problem is not knowing how to cope with, express, or manage how they feel. It's that they likely don't know how to self-regulate their emotions or make healthy choices and decisions.

Drugs and alcohol are your loved one's *solution* to the problem they don't know how else to solve, and along the way, their brain rewired itself to make it nearly impossible for them to stop.

Nobody sets out to become an alcoholic or an addict. Nobody who becomes one wants to be one. By the time someone becomes an addict, the choice is no longer in their hands. They can't think their way out of it or will their way out of it, but that's exactly what they're expected to do because the real problem isn't being understood, acknowledged, and addressed.

You can't muster up willingness from an empty shell. Willingness implies there is some desire for something better, some sense of self-worth and inner resilience. For most as addiction progresses, self-worth dwindles and eventually is completely gone.

The sooner you, as a loved one of someone with addiction, grasp that their problem is not the drugs and alcohol, the sooner you can get to the real solution. Right now, both of you are fighting different battles: they are fighting to cope with their inside pain, and you are fighting their behavior and resource of choice. Their behavior only represents the *symptoms* of addiction, and treating those alone does nothing to solve the real problem. Until you fully understand this, you're going to spiral further into the chaos that addiction wants you in, fighting a losing battle.

TOUCHING AGAIN ON CHOICE

When it comes to the stigma around addiction, I see two main causes. The first is the symptoms of addiction, which we'll dig into next in this chapter. The second is the perception that continuing to drink or use drugs is a choice.

I said in the previous chapter that you are always at choice. Someone in active addiction is not. Not when it comes to their addiction.

Their brain has been hijacked to the point where their logical, rational brain is no longer able to communicate with the "animal" brain that controls survival instinct, and their survival instinct is screaming to drink/use drugs in order to stay alive.

Telling them to stop and expecting them to do it would be like telling you to stop breathing and wondering why you can't. After a certain point, it's out of your control.

What adds to this stigma is that someone might be sober when they take a drink. Therefore, they chose to do it, right? It's more complicated than that. Being sober is not the same as being in recovery, and relapses often happen emotionally and mentally before a chemical relapse. We'll dive into that more later on in this chapter as well, so keep reading.

But, please know that your loved one isn't choosing their addiction; they are being held hostage by it.

Spotting the Symptoms of Addiction

One of the first ways I teach families to start creating change is to pay attention to who's talking when their loved one is speaking. Is it their addiction, or is it recovery? Because if it's their addiction talking, there's no rationalizing with it, but if it's recovery, then there's a chance for connection.

So, what does addiction look and sound like?

Addiction looks like lying, denying, justifying, rationalizing, minimizing, compartmentalizing, blaming, criticizing, avoiding, and complaining.

Let me give you an example from when I was active in my addiction:

I had stayed sober for two weeks before relapsing. At this point, I had already told my kids, who were fifteen, eighteen, and twenty-one at the time, that I was an alcoholic. One day, I walked into my house, a large Dunkin' Donuts cup filled with chardonnay in my hand, to find them waiting for me around the kitchen table. Lined up on the table in front of them were eight empty wine bottles they had found on my closet floor.

I immediately got defensive. "What?" I demanded.

They said, "We just found these in your closet."

"Those are from a long time ago."

My youngest daughter said, "No they're not, Mom. They weren't there last week."

And I said, "Well, what do you want from me?"

Inside my head at that moment was a running dialogue with one voice asking myself, "*What are you doing?!*" The other voice demanded, "*How dare they speak to their mom that way?*"

The words I had wanted to say out loud that I vividly remember being stuck in my throat were, "*Please, help me,*" but every time I tried to say them, I literally felt like a hand went over my mouth. The thing that came out instead was, "I think you guys are being pretty disrespectful, speaking to your mom like that."

These were my babies, whom I would die for, confronting me because they loved me. They were scared and mad, and they wanted me to get better. They wanted the madness to stop, and all I was able to see at that moment was the half a glass of wine still left in the bottom of one of the bottles. All that was speaking was my addiction. I was aware this conflict was happening inside of me, but I did not know why, and I did not know what to do about it. It was scary, and it was sad.

Did you spot the symptoms of addiction in that story?

The way I lied about the bottles being old and denied I'd relapsed. How I criticized my kids for calling me out, turning all the blame and responsibility off of myself to avoid confronting the truth. All of which my kids probably took as me choosing the wine over them. After all, I'd already admitted to them I was an alcoholic. If I knew I had a problem, shouldn't I have been able to stop? Not yet understanding addiction themselves, they probably thought so.

It's because of how I talked to my kids during my addiction that it's so important to me for you to know when the addiction is speaking. You'll think your loved one doesn't care about you, but I promise you they do. Anything that comes out of your loved one's mouth that falls under this list of symptoms is the addiction talking. I'd go so far as to say that anything that falls out of their mouth that comes from a place of hate or fear rather than love is the addiction speaking.

So when you hear these things, rather than let them in and accept them as fact and try to argue with them, the goal is to get to the point where you're able to take a step back just enough to be able to see that they aren't the truth; they're the sickness.

This is not so simple to do, especially while in the moment. What I suggest is that as often as you can as you continue to learn about addiction and begin to untangle from its effect on you, remind yourself of the following:

- ❖ It's the addiction doing most (if not all) of your loved one's talking.
- ❖ Your loved one's addiction is not who they are.
- ❖ Addiction thrives in the dark, and it will try to smother you in the dark as well through anger, hurt, and lies.

Recovery, on the other hand, sounds like honesty, open-mindedness, accepting responsibility, willingness, compassion, patience, peace, and love.

Depending on how far your loved one has progressed in their addiction, you may not be seeing or hearing much of this list anymore. Please know it is there. Where there is breath, there is a part of them—it might be a really, really small part, but I promise it's there—that wants to be willing, that wants to be honest, that has forgotten how to care, and that is fighting to be compassionate toward you *and* toward themselves. But in order to do that, we as addicts have to find the part of ourselves that we care about first, the part that is buried under the addiction, and when you're using a needle to shoot fentanyl or heroin into your body, when you're downing a fifth of alcohol just to wake up, you don't have easy access to the part of you that cares about yourself. That doesn't mean you never will.

LEARN WHAT RECOVERY LOOKS LIKE

The best way to learn what recovery looks like, and to increase your feelings of hope for your loved one to recover, is to listen to those who are recovering. There are several ways you can do this:

- Go to open AA meetings. While closed meetings are restricted to those who identify as the alcoholic, nonalcoholics may attend open meetings as observers. Find a meeting in your area or online, go, and listen. (For more information, check out the Additional Resources section in the back of this book.)

- Search for "AA Speaker" on YouTube. Hundreds of results will show up of people in recovery sharing their stories.

- Join our membership program where we have a different guest speaker each month. (To learn more, schedule a call with us at https://tippingpointrecovery. as.me/connection-call.)

- Attend our Double Circle Meeting, which is open to both the person who identifies as the addict as well as those who identify as family and friends.

As you listen to more and more recovery stories, pay attention to the similarities. Keep an ear out for when you hear the speakers being honest and accepting responsibility for their actions. Notice when they express willingness, compassion, and patience. The more you do this, the more automatic recognizing recovery will become, which will make it that much easier to spot when it's addiction showing up instead.

Recovery vs. Sobriety

The last thing I want to touch on in this chapter is the difference between recovery and sobriety for a couple of reasons: (a) because they're often confused as being the same thing, and (b) because understanding the difference helps to drive home the point that addiction is not about the drugs and alcohol.

There's a saying I learned in recovery that goes, "take away the alcohol and you still have the 'ick.'"

If you've ever heard the term "dry drunk," this is what it means. The person isn't drinking—they're sober—but they're still sick. By taking away the alcohol, all that's happened is their solution (to coping with the pain and difficulty that has become their life) has been removed. Everything inside

100

is still the same or may be even worse. While they may display fewer symptoms that the drugs and alcohol amplified, they're still left with the underlying problem.

To see what I mean, try spending time with someone who's just stopped using drugs and alcohol but isn't working a recovery program. It's apparent they aren't healthy. They still have the "ick."

This is because sobriety is not the same as recovery.

To be sober is simply to be abstinent from drugs and alcohol. To be in recovery is to do the inner work of identifying and understanding your "ick" and then learning the tools to clean it up. Tools to help you take responsibility, tools to help you make better decisions, tools to help you learn to cope with feelings, and tools to help you make amends and do the next right thing.

In fact, you as the loved one of someone with an addiction likely have your own "ick" despite not being addicted to a substance. Actually, I'm certain you do (because everyone does), and being aware of it is just as important for you as it is for your loved one. We'll dive into it together in the next chapter.

KEY CHAPTER
TAKEAWAYS

❖ Addiction is a complex illness and not one that anyone chooses.

❖ The underlying problem for those with substance use disorder is *not* the drugs and alcohol. The real problem is the anxiety, depression, mood and/or other inner disorders they are self-medicating with drugs and alcohol as their solution.

❖ The symptoms of addiction are lying, denying, justifying, rationalizing, minimizing, compartmentalizing, blaming, criticizing, and complaining.

❖ Recovery, on the other hand, looks like honesty, open-mindedness, personal responsibility, acceptance, willingness, compassion, patience, peace, and love.

❖ Sobriety is not the same as recovery. Sobriety is simply abstinence from substances while recovery is working a program to address the underlying problem.

❖ Take away the alcohol and you still have the "ick."

CHAPTER 7
WHAT'S YOUR LOOP?

In the last chapter, we looked at how the disease of addiction has made your loved one unwell and has them trapped in a cycle of self-medicating. At this point, I want to invite you to reflect on the ways *you* have become unwell as a result of loving someone struggling with drug or alcohol addiction.

I want to preface this by saying that this chapter of the framework is where some families start to come up against their own resistance. It's a lot harder to look inward at your own stuff than it is pointing to someone else's, and the deeper you dive, the more you may end up feeling things that are uncomfortable or be faced with truths you'd rather not confront.

Recovery, for you and your loved one, is about working through and moving beyond that discomfort.

Remember, avoidance is a symptom of addiction, so instead of pulling back when you encounter resistance, I invite you to try to sit with it. Get curious about it. Look at it and lean in. Explore where it is coming from, and be gentle with yourself. You can take some deep breaths and revisit it.

Healing isn't always easy, but I promise it's worth it.

Finding Your Loop

Just like your loved one is self-medicating and seeking ways to cover up their internal struggles with drugs and alcohol, you are trying to cover up and smooth over your fear, confusion, sadness, worry, etc. Unlike your loved one, you may not be using substances to do it.

So, what are you using?

To find the answer to that question, we have to look a little closer at the pain itself.

Maybe you feel angry when your loved one lies to you about being at work when they are really off somewhere drinking.

Maybe you feel scared when your loved one relapses because the last time landed them in the hospital.

Maybe you feel helpless when you know your loved one is using again because nothing you did before to get them to stop seemed to make a difference.

Maybe you feel worried that your loved one who has been in recovery for a few months is going to relapse because they've not experienced this much recovery before, and you're just waiting for the other shoe to drop.

Whatever your pain, you likely do something in response to it to try and relieve that discomfort. It could be that you call their job to get proof they weren't there and then yell at them for it. Maybe you try to bribe them back into recovery or you shut them out altogether, ignoring what's happening rather than facing it again.

Clients of mine have admitted to spying on their loved one's phone to check their Uber account and see if they went to the liquor store. They've followed their loved one in their car and parked outside their house to keep an eye on them. They've slipped into caregiver mode, buying their loved one new clothes, cooking them food, or cleaning their apartment all in an attempt to *will* them into being better.

It's important to identify these behaviors for what they are: coping strategies seeking to soothe your discomfort in the face of your loved one's addiction, because let's face it, witnessing a loved one in their addiction is horrendous.

It's confusing.

It's maddening.

It's heartbreaking.

It's all those things.

But, just like their self-medication with drugs and alcohol isn't helping them, these actions you've come to rely on as coping mechanisms for your own discomfort are not helping you.

They are keeping you stuck in your own unwell loop.

Here's how it goes:

Something happens with your loved one—maybe they relapse or get a DUI or experience a breakup—and it spikes your fear response. That discomfort you experience leads you to act out in an attempt to fix it, pay for it, and/or cover it up. For a moment, what you do seems to help. At the very least, it's a distraction from your pain, something you can do to feel like you're being helpful, to feel like you're in control.

Only, instead of solving anything, your actions backfire. Instead of your loved one admitting to skipping work when you confront them, you end up getting into a shouting match and they storm out. Instead of keeping them sober by exerting all your time and energy tracking their whereabouts, they're still drinking, only now you're sleep deprived, which drives your anxiety higher. Instead of the chaos easing, it has intensified.

This is exhausting.

These consequences of you acting out lead to more discomfort, and that discomfort leads you to act out again only to experience temporary relief before more consequences surface...

And you're caught in a loop just like your loved one.

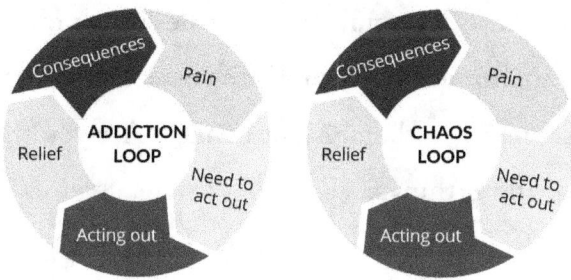

What you end up with is two people, like two spinning wheels side by side, each spiraling into your own chaos, unable to connect with one another.

This does not lead to recovery.

It's just sick feeding sick, perpetuating the problem despite it being the last thing you intended.

One of you has to start to get healthy for this pattern to change, and of the two of you, *you*—whoever is reading this book right now—*you* are the one with the best chance of breaking this cycle.

You can begin this process.

Start by thinking about what it is you do when you're trying to avoid the discomfort you feel. Another way to ask that is, **what is something you are doing in response to your loved one's addiction that is no longer serving you?** What do you do that is actually contributing to your own chaos rather than relieving it?

You could also ask yourself, **what roles have you taken on that you are not qualified for?** Are you acting as your loved one's case manager, therapist, or banker? Are you trained to do any of those things? (Even if you are, chances are your ability to do it is compromised by your close relationship with your loved one. There is a reason surgeons don't operate on their family members.)

That's your loop.

Here are a few common loops we see our clients stuck in when they first come to us:

The Obsessor	The Case Manager	The Caretaker	The Worrier
Pain: You suspect your loved one is drinking.	**Pain:** Your loved one isn't taking steps to get sober.	**Pain:** Your loved one needs a job, a place to live, money for food, etc.	**Pain:** You haven't heard from your loved one in a few days.

Need to act out: You need/want to know for sure.	Need to act out: You are determined to get them into treatment.	Need to act out: You feel the need to take care of these things.	Need to act out: Your brain starts running through worst-case scenarios; you need to know they're okay.
Acting out: You track their phone, search their room, and hunt for proof.	**Acting out:** You make it your responsibility to find a treatment center and make the arrangements, and then you use ultimatums to pressure your loved one to go.	**Acting out:** You search for jobs they can apply for, buy them groceries, drive them to appointments, and pay their first and last month's rent.	**Acting out:** You call and text them several times, seeking details about how they are doing.
Temporary relief: You either experience validation that you were right in your suspicions or relief that at least for now they seem to be sober.	**Temporary relief:** You feel a sense of control over the situation.	**Temporary relief:** You feel like you're helping them get back on their feet so they can get sober. Now that these things are handled, you think they'll find recovery.	**Temporary relief:** You can relax, knowing they're alive and safe (for now).

Consequences of acting out: You feel unsettled about the way your actions spiraled, and your loved one is angry with you for violating their privacy, creating more distrust in your relationship.	Consequences of acting out: You've run yourself ragged trying to find a silver bullet. Your loved one backs out of the arrangement (or never intended to go in the first place), putting you right back where you started.	Consequences of acting out: In dedicating all of your focus and energy on them, you've lost sight of yourself, and none of it stops them from drinking/using or allows for recovery. In fact, their addiction often progresses.	Consequences of acting out: Your wellness is contingent on how they are doing, and you find yourself missing when your relationship was about more than just their addiction. They're annoyed by your overstepping and start to pull back, reaching out to you less and less.

You may find you have more than one loop, or your loop may change depending on where your loved one is at in their recovery. Ultimately, the goal in identifying your loop, however many there are, is to start to be able to break it by shifting into a healthier cycle of responding to your pain.

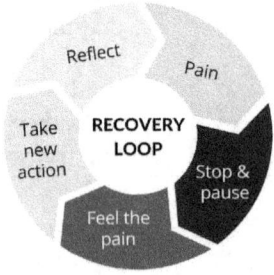

In this new cycle, when something happens with your loved one—they relapse, get a DUI, or experience a break-up—the very first thing I suggest you do is stop and pause. Stop everything you are doing in that moment so you can take some deep breaths, allow the emotion to move through you, and pause on taking action until you can do so from a more grounded place.

This next part is difficult but crucial. Let yourself feel the pain and *lean into* it.

Do you feel worried right now? Angry? Helpless? What sensations are you experiencing in your body? Is your heart racing? Are your muscles straining to *go, act, and run?*

Take more deep breaths. Place your hand over your racing heart. Say what you're feeling out loud. Put a name to it. Then, and only then as you are feeling yourself drop in, decide what you want to do differently. (We'll dive into the specifics of our decision-making blueprint in the next chapter.)

Once you've taken the steps to not react as you used to, take a moment to make note of this change. It is not easy to create change. I celebrate you!

Then, reflect on the experience of taking new action:

❖ What changes do you see in this experience from how things have gone in the past?

❖ How are you thinking differently?

❖ How do you feel different?

The changes may be subtle or they may feel monumental. Either way, they're worth acknowledging and honoring. Pausing and celebrating your small steps allows for the change to be anchored in.

Now, breaking loops that have been automatic behaviors for what has likely been years isn't something that happens overnight. It's best to take this in stages, and the first stage I recommend is to detox.

Time to Detox

What's the first thing someone in active addiction needs to do when they want to begin to recover? They withdraw from their substance use and detox. After you identify your own loop, I'm going to invite you to do the same. Detox for at least seventy-two hours from whatever obsessive action, activity, behavior, pattern of thinking, etc., is no longer serving you.

Maybe that's monitoring your loved one's phone or searching their room for booze. It could be tracking their schedule so you can remind them of their own responsibilities. Or maybe it's an unhelpful thought—like that you are responsible for whether or not they drink. (You're not!) Whatever it is, try to set it down and step away for seventy-two hours.

If you feel moved to detox for longer than seventy-two hours, by all means do it! The goal is to stop this unhelpful behavior permanently. For most, setting a shorter time frame on it makes it more palpable.

Now unlike your loved one, you won't be going away to a facility to detox with comfort meds and under the supervision of others. (Though, doing it inside a recovery community, like the kind available in our programs where you have peers, tools and mentors at hand to help you through the ups and downs, significantly supports the process.) So, how do you go about detoxing on your own?

Here are some suggestions for a successful detox:

1. **Set your intention.** Decide what you are detoxing from and set the intention to do it. This could be as simple as stating it out loud or writing it out in your journal. "I'm committing to detoxing from _____ for seventy-two hours. This behavior is no longer serving me."

2. **Tell someone about your detox.** Share with someone close to you what you are detoxing from. Put it out there.

This could be another family member, a close friend, or someone at a recovery meeting. If you attend our Double Circle Meeting (https://www.tippingpointrecovery.com/recovery-meeting/), share it here. Or, you can join our Friends of Tipping Point online community (https://www.facebook.com/groups/friendsoftippingpoint) and make a post about it.

3. **Reflect on the experience.** At the end of each day, journal about what the detox was like for you that day. Was it hard to stop? Did you drop right back into your loop again? How did you feel throughout the experience? What came up for you? Try not to judge or criticize yourself for any of it; simply observe.

Something important to note before you get started:

You will very likely relapse.

Before the first day (or hour) of your detox is through, you will likely fall back into your loop, and you might do it without even realizing it. I remember a time when I was driving by a liquor store when I was ten days sober. I wanted to be recovered like nobody's business; I was determined. Before I knew it, I was standing at the register holding a bottle in my hand.

Later on when I was in recovery from addiction and in a relationship with an active addict, I'd commit myself to stop spiraling into his chaos only to catch myself out of breath with anger before realizing what had triggered that anger in the first place.

Sometimes you relapse and you're not even aware that you're already in it. It's okay. The goal isn't to beat yourself up for relapsing and doing the thing you're trying to detox from. The goal is to say, "Whoa, baby. Check it out. I just did that thing." Give yourself some grace.

Stopping these habits you've been using to try to cope for years—habits that have become hardwired into your brain to the point that they're instinctual—isn't easy just like your loved one learning to cope without substances isn't easy. The process really is the same for you both. It would be nice if you both could just detox once and for all and never have to worry about it again, but that's usually not how it works.

That doesn't mean it's not worth it to try. Just the opposite. Because even if you relapse, the awareness and the peace of mind that can come from catching yourself, taking a deep breath, and realizing, "Wow, I just really spun out," is key to catching yourself sooner the next time.

Find Your Lane

There's a saying I learned during my own recovery that goes, "There's my business, and there's none of my business."

Chances are, your fear and anger for your loved one has had you all up in their business. So much so that you probably don't even realize just how much.

You're like two balls of yarn all tangled up together into one messy knot where you can't even find where one of you ends and the other begins. Their problems become your problems. Their feelings become your feelings. Their responsibilities become your responsibilities. Some call it enmeshment. I like to call it entangled.

That entanglement is not healthy for either of you. It can end up keeping you in their chaos and may even get to the point that it prevents them from finding their own path.

The goal is to untangle yourself from them so that you can find where you end and they begin. It's so the two of you can walk side by side, without tripping over each other or dragging one another down.

You in your lane. Them in their lane.

Because—and I really need you to hear this—your loved one's recovery is not your job.

I'll say it again: **your loved one's recovery is not your job**.

Just like your recovery is not your loved one's job. Your feelings are not their responsibility. Those are for you to manage just like what they feel is for them to manage. Being in your own lane, on your own recovery path, allows you to heal, and it gives your loved one the space to heal themselves.

Because that's the thing about entanglement. When you're all up in their lane, you don't just burden yourself with their stuff; you also dump *your* stuff all over *their* path, and I am pretty sure you don't want to do that. You don't want to give them even more to manage. Keep your stuff in your lane so they have one less thing to step over on their journey toward recovery.

To help you get a handle on this, I'm going to walk you through the exercise I do with families to help them distinguish what's theirs and what's their loved one's.

Finding Your Lane Exercise

On a piece of paper, draw a line down the center to create two columns. Label the left column "Mine" and the right column "Theirs." Now, on a separate piece of paper (or typed out on the computer—just somewhere you can see the words in front of you), write out a situation involving your loved one where you got caught up in it. Maybe you were frustrated by it, were worried, tried to control it, or fell back into your loop—you got caught up in the chaos in some way. Take a moment to write out what happened in a few sentences as if you were telling it to a friend or posting it in our Facebook group.

When you're done, go through your paragraph line by line, word by word, and write down anything that's yours in the "Mine" column and anything that's your loved one's in the "Theirs" column. Your feelings, thoughts, beliefs, and actions are yours. Their feelings, thoughts, beliefs, and actions are theirs.

Here's what it looks like.

Example #1:

"Last week, I was so mad that my son wrecked another vehicle. This is car number five in less than two years. His father was three hours away. I was one hour away. His father called me to tell me what happened and told me I needed to leave my house right now and go up to the accident site to get my son's tools out of his truck."

Let's break this down:

"Last week I was so mad that my son wrecked another vehicle." — "I was so mad" is this mother's. That would go under the "Mine" column. "My son wrecked another vehicle" is her son's. That goes under "Theirs."

"This is car number five in less than two years. His father was three hours away. I was one hour away." — This is context for the story and doesn't need to go into a column.

"His father called me to tell me what happened and told me I needed to leave my house right now and go up to the accident site to get my son's tools out of his truck." — "His father called me to tell me what happened" goes under "Mine" because the mother chose to answer the phone, so that's on her. "Told me I needed to leave my house right now and go up to the accident site to get my son's tools out of his truck" is another way of saying, "My son needed his tools from his truck." That's her son's problem, not hers. What *is* hers is whether she decides to make it her problem by driving the hour to get the tools.

Example #2:

"Our daughter called tonight to let us know she'd relapsed and was kicked out of her sober home. She had no place to go and wanted us to let her come home. We said no and tried to do so with love, but she got very angry, swore, and said she would have to end up on the streets. We encouraged her to reach out to recovery and social service resources she knows of. We are worried that she will show up on our doorstep and we'll have to deal with a confrontation."

The breakdown:

"Our daughter relapsed and was kicked out of her sober home." — Hers.

"She had no place to go and wanted us to let her come home." — Hers.

"We said no and tried to do so with love" — The parents' (Mine).

"But she got very angry, swore, and said she would have to end up on the streets." — Hers.

"We encouraged her to reach out to recovery services…" — The parents' (Mine).

"We are worried that she will end up on our doorstep and we'll have to deal with a confrontation." — The parents' (Mine).

The last example I want to briefly mention is a mom who called me to tell me her son had overdosed and was in jail. Personally as his recovery coach, I was relieved because it meant he was alive and safe at the moment. A stint in jail can also offer a chance for reflection and often increases the potential for thoughts such as "maybe I want to do things differently."

This mom, though, was so devastated, which of course made perfect sense. She thought about her boy being in jail and was so scared for him. She worried he'd be cold, worried he'd be scared and sad, worried about him having a felony to deal with, worried about fines to pay, and all the other complications that come from being in jail. It's a lot.

But all those feelings? That worry and that fear? Those feelings are *hers* to manage. While her son was in jail, I encouraged her to explore those feelings separate from him. She worked to not put any of her feelings on him whenever she spoke to him or visited him. As she was in her own lane managing her feelings, her son could experience the consequences of his actions in his lane. Experiencing those consequences on his own without the weight of his mom's emotions or the cushion of her helping him out made it more likely he'd consider doing something about those consequences. In fact, I've yet to meet an addict who went to jail and didn't have it impact their increased willingness to recover.

So, now it's your turn. Write out a scenario you've experienced with your loved one and pull out what's yours and what's theirs. Keep practicing this exercise as situations arise. The more you do it, the quicker you'll become at catching yourself when you step outside of your own lane and the easier it will become to get back into it.

Once you are grounded in your own lane, that's when you can begin to make recovery-oriented decisions that will allow you to take new action. Join me in the next chapter to learn how.

KEY CHAPTER TAKEAWAYS

❖ Just like your loved one is caught in a loop of self-medicating their discomfort, you are caught in a similar loop that is unhealthy for you and may even perpetuate the problem further.

❖ Breaking yourself of your own loop is a powerful step you can take toward recovery for yourself and your family, and it starts with identifying which of your actions in response to your loved one's addiction no longer serve you. What role can you resign or fire yourself from?

❖ Your loved one's recovery is not your job. Your recovery is not your loved one's job. The goal is for you both to walk on your own paths alongside each other, you in your lane and them in theirs.

❖ Writing down situations that have happened with your loved one that left you upset, frazzled, or overwhelmed can be helpful in sorting out what from that situation is yours to manage and what is your loved one's.

CHAPTER 8
DECISION-MAKING BLUEPRINT

At this point in the book, you are really starting to understand that your loved one's loop and your loop are separate. You may not fully be out of your loved one's lane yet or know exactly what your own loop is, and you may not be fully clear on what's yours and what's theirs, but you at least understand that the two lanes are separate things.

From here, it's a matter of having a system in place for making the decisions that keep you in your recovery lane, because remember—you walking your recovery path increases your loved one's bandwidth to access theirs.

Recovery-Oriented Decisions

This decision-making blueprint is about making decisions from a place of love rather than fear, recovery-oriented decisions rather than addiction-driven ones.

Here's what makes a decision recovery-oriented:

1. It's made from a grounded place within your own recovery lane that aligns with your values and standards.
2. It's motivated by love and health rather than fear and avoidance.
3. It in no way supports the addiction, only recovery, and thereby allows for your loved one's best chance of success.

Addiction-driven decisions, on the other hand, are reactions triggered by fear, pain, confusion, and anger that feed right back into the chaos loops we want to break.

Now, this doesn't all have to happen in a straight line. You can still start putting this decision-making blueprint to use even if you aren't fully in your own lane.

Everyone's journey is different, and no one is going to read this and then snap their fingers and instantly be in their own lane. You have developed these habits and patterns of interacting with your loved one over years and years. It's going to take time to unlearn that and be able to not only find your lane but reside there. Try to manage those expectations and have grace with yourself as you navigate.

Step #1: Get Present

In order to be grounded in your own lane, you need to be able to recognize when you've wandered into someone else's. It's hard to do that when you're in hyperdrive.

More often than not, our addiction-driven decisions are made as knee-jerk reactions triggered by a sense of urgency and panic; a feeling like you have to do something *now* before it gets worse or becomes too late. But that rushing leaves no room for clarity. It gives you no time to determine if what you're doing will actually help or will only serve the addiction.

That is why getting present and grounded in your body is the crucial first step.

The 3 Keys to Getting Grounded

1. **Pause & Breathe**

   The very first thing you should do any time you don't know what to do is pause.

   Literally, wherever you are, whatever you are doing, pause, ground yourself, and breathe. Put your hand on your belly and close your eyes. Feel your stomach expand as you breathe in deep and feel it contract as you exhale it all out. Do that at least three times. Depending on what's going on around you, you may need to do this fifty times a day. Do it as many times as you need.

2. Regulate Your Nervous System

There are several techniques you can choose from to do this. Tapping, or ETF, is one that I've linked introductory training videos to in the resource section at the end of this book. You could touch every finger of your hand to your thumb—1-2-3-4, 1-2-3-4, etc. You could focus on your five senses by asking yourself, "What can I see, smell, hear, touch, and taste right now?" Do whatever will bring you out of your head and down into your body.

3. Talk to Someone

Not just any someone. I'm going to encourage you to not call the friend that tends to get you riled up and who cosigns the story with you. Years ago, I had friends who served this role. We would commiserate together about frustrations, and it only led to more spiraling, which is the opposite of what we want to accomplish here. So instead, think of someone that you could check in with (ideally also in recovery) who is going to help you get grounded. If you're in our member community, we direct you to the private Facebook group for this. Our community is here so you can support each other as you navigate these situations. Take advantage of it.

If you aren't a member yet but are interested in learning about what programs are available to you, go ahead and schedule a call to chat here: https://tippingpointrecovery. as.me/connection-call

Step #2: What's Your Intention?

Imagine your loved one is at treatment and they call you saying there are bedbugs, the food is terrible, someone is trying to hurt them, they hate it there, come get them. You don't really think you should, but the next thing you know you're in your car driving to go pick them up. You catch yourself midway through carrying out this decision that you don't even know if you should make.

Step #1 of this decision-making process is to pause, so you find a safe place to pull over your car and just sit there and breathe. You listen to the cars driving past on the road until your body has relaxed a little and your grip is somewhat looser on the steering wheel.

Now, you want to ask yourself, "What is my intention here? What do I want to happen?" It's important that you are really honest with yourself here because sometimes the answer to those two questions isn't the same.

Like in this example, your intention behind going to pick your loved one up is to ease their (and your) discomfort, but what you actually want to happen is for them to stay in treatment.

Both are important to get clear on. Go ahead and write them down if it helps you work through this process, especially as you first start practicing it.

Step #3: What Action Do You Want to Take?

What are you thinking of doing? Do you want to keep driving to pick them up? Do you want to turn around and go home? Whichever it is you are leaning toward, ask yourself *why?*

Think back to what I said in Chapter 5 about choices and understanding your reasons and motivations behind them. What is at the root of the choice you are thinking of making? *Why* do you want to make that choice?

You aren't actually making the decision either way yet; you're just getting clear on what it is you *want* to do.

Step #4: Does This Action Feed the Addiction?

Look at your answer from Step #3 and ask yourself, "Does this action feed recovery (love) or does it feed the addiction (fear)?"

For example, if the reason you want to keep driving to pick them up is because you're *afraid* that if you don't, they'll check themselves out and you won't know where they are anymore, that's acting out of fear. That's potentially feeding the addiction. That's the old way of feeding "what if."

This example scenario is actually based off of a mom I once worked with who called me an hour and a half into a three-hour drive to pick her son up from treatment after he'd called. The drive had given her enough time to realize she was reacting rather than responding, and she called me to help her sort through her decision. We ended up creating a boundary for her to use, and then she continued her work with me through developing a family contract.

That's the new way. Getting to a meeting, calling your sponsor, or talking to a professional to help you make a re-covery-oriented decision that is rooted in love.

If you're in our membership, this would be when you post in the Facebook group and ask for advice. Seek out your peers, your teachers, your recovery coach, or your therapist.

Turn to your recovery community. (I'll go into more detail about how to find your recovery community in a later chapter.) Let them help remind you where your lane is and what actions you can take that feed the recovery.

If you get put on the spot by your loved one and feel like you need to make a split-second decision, a possible reply could be, "That's a great question. Let me get back to you." This will buy you the time and space you need to get advice, make a plan, and put this decision-making blueprint in action. (This is a disarming statement, and we give you more of them in the next chapter.)

Remember to have grace for yourself. This is really hard. It's something a lot of our clients struggle with because oftentimes making a recovery-oriented decision means letting your loved one stay in their discomfort while leaning into your own.

Doing things differently means caring about their (and your) recovery more than their feelings about what you are or aren't doing.

What your loved one is taught in treatment is they only need to change one thing: everything. You are part of their everything which means in order for them to have the best chance of recovery, you need to change as well.

That's your ultimate choice: "Am I willing to change?"

If you made it this far in the book, I'm betting your answer is yes. If you choose to walk this recovery path, I'm confident you won't regret it. None of the families we work with do because it leads to a healthier life, one you get to thrive in.

When you thrive from a place of recovery, standing solid in your lane and making recovery-oriented decisions, you become a resource for recovery, offering your loved one the absolute best chance of success.

KEY CHAPTER
TAKEAWAYS

❖ Having a decision-making blueprint in place is the easiest way to make sure you are making grounded decisions from your own lane.

❖ The goal is to make recovery-oriented decisions based in love rather than addiction-driven decisions rooted in fear. Addiction-driven decisions tend to be impulsive reactions whereas recovery-oriented decisions are made from a grounded place in your own lane using a decision-making process.

❖ There are four steps to the decision-making blueprint:

- 1. Get present
- 2. What's your intention?
- 3. What action do you want to take?
- 4. Does this action feed the addiction?

PART
03

WALKING A
RECOVERY PATH

CHAPTER 9
RECOVERY CONVERSATIONS™

Picture yourself standing at a fork in the road with two paths laid out before you. To the left is the path you've been walking till now, the one where you're stuck in a loop, doing things that you hope are helpful or that have simply become your norm, and so you keep doing them despite nothing getting better. It's the path of chaos, the path of fear, and the path of addiction.

The path to the right is a new path, one where you can start to do things differently. That's the path toward recovery.

Just by reading this book, you've already started to take a step on your recovery path. You've stood at the fork in the road and decided to turn away from the path you've been wandering and to look in a different direction. You've decided to think about (or likely already are!) doing something different. In this chapter, I'm going to lay out several more steps you can take, and keep taking, to continue on your recovery journey.

If there's one thing I want you to understand when it comes to walking a recovery path, it's that this journey has no finish line. Recovery isn't a goal that you achieve once and leave behind. It's a forever journey. You're either walking the path of recovery or you're not.

It's a decision. One you make daily to continue down the path of recovery instead of veering back in the other direction. And if you backtrack? That's okay. That's part of the journey too.

It's not a straight line. Sometimes we stumble. Sometimes we get turned around. Sometimes we think we're going one way and end up someplace we didn't expect. The beauty of having tools like this **Dear Family Framework** is that you can pull them out when you need them to get back on a healthier track.

It's important to note that I'm not teaching you these steps so you can go and teach them to your loved one.

You taking what you've learned and bringing it to your loved one is like you trying to stop them from drinking. It slips you right back into the loop of trying to convince them to change and rationalize with their addiction when addiction *can't* be rationalized with. To try to stop addiction is like trying to stop the rain.

This is about you starting to recover yourself because you deserve it and because recovery is contagious. It's about you changing the steps of the dance so your loved one has the opportunity to change theirs.

However, I also don't want you walking around on eggshells. I don't want you worrying or obsessing over whether or not you do this right. This is simply about showing you a different path to take. If you recognize that what you've been doing up till now isn't working, you can become willing to learn a new way.

We'll start with a whole new way of communicating.

Say This, Not That

Family recovery, in a sense, is about learning a whole new language.

It's sort of like addiction is a foreign country and your loved one is speaking to you, but you can't understand what they are really saying because you don't speak the language. What you need is an interpreter, and that's where I come in.

The first thing you need to understand is that there are two parts to your loved one: their true self and their addicted self.

When your loved one is active in their addiction, their addiction is likely doing most (if not all) of the talking: the lying, denying, and justifying, the nasty remarks and hurtful comments meant to manipulate and guilt you. Yet there are moments when their true self will manage to peek through. It's helpful to learn to recognize when it's the addiction talking and when it's their true self talking because knowing which one it is will determine how you respond.

Your loved one is not their addiction.

Their addiction is *in* them. It's in their hearts, in their minds, and in their actions, but it is not *who* they are. By differentiating how you respond to your loved one from how you respond to their addiction, you extend and increase compassion and respect for their true self while turning away from the addiction frequency they are stuck in.

What's been going on up until now in your interactions with your loved one is they have been predominantly speaking through their addiction, and you've been meeting them there with your feelings that are (naturally) fueled by fear, anger, confusion, and pain. By understanding addiction and changing how you respond, you can step out of the frequency of the addiction and help them meet you in your grounded recovery conversation, one rooted in love.

Keep in mind that just because you speak to your loved one in a more loving way does not mean you shouldn't feel mad. You still get to feel all your feelings. It's just about where you choose to put those feelings and where and how you process them. Take your anger and bring it to a recovery meeting, bring it to your therapist, bring it to our private membership Facebook group, and let it all out in the safety of those containers. The goal isn't to deny your pain. It's to avoid throwing that pain at your loved one, because no one heals that way.

Also, keep in mind that you speaking to them in a loving way does not mean you will get a loving response back. You almost certainly won't if your loved one is active in their addiction, but chances are high that their reaction will be different. You can learn to manage yourself, not their response to you.

I get regular emails and texts from clients saying, "You're not gonna believe what just happened. I responded the way you suggested and it was completely different." That will be your experience as well. It might not happen immediately, but it will happen eventually.

So, what should you say?

I recommend having a few go-to statements on hand that you can use at any time for any situation. They are disarming statements, and the idea is to use them when you notice yourself feeling scared, worried, or overwhelmed—generally caught up in the chaos—as a way of giving yourself the time and space to pause, breathe, and really think about your response.

I mentioned one disarming statement as an example in the last chapter: "That's a great question. Let me get back to you." This kind of reply will likely cause your loved one to feel a different energy from you, and it will show them you are in recovery and are done living in chaos. It's also kind, truthful, and not emotionally charged, lacking any glimpse of shame or blame.

Here are a few more of my favorites:

Disarming Statements

1. "Let me think about that and get back to you."
2. "The old me would have said _____; the new me wants to do everything differently."
3. "That may be true."
4. "I can only talk for a few minutes right now. What's up?"
5. "Great question. I'm going to call my sponsor and I'll call you back."

6. "I love you and no."

7. "Hmmm."

Having a statement like this on hand allows you to stop and pause rather than react. If they ask you for money? You can respond, "Let me think about that and get back to you." Then, go call your sponsor, therapist, or recovery coach to help you navigate what you want to do.

If they try to get sympathy for how bad things are for them right now and how no one cares? You can nod in empathy and give a simple, "Mmmm, I love you." That's it. You're not denying their experience or shutting them out, but you're also not hooking into the addiction.

Take a look at the columns below for more examples of ways to potentially shift your responses using recovery language.

Instead of saying...	Try...
"You should go to a meeting." "Have you been going to meetings?"	"I just went to a recovery meeting and had to share, and it was really uncomfortable. I can understand how hard this is." "I've got to get to a meeting." (You can also add, "Do you want to come?")
"You need to call your sponsor."	"I'm going to call my sponsor to talk this through. I'll get back to you."

"Just stop and listen to what I have to say."	"I'm feeling a certain way about our interaction last night (or whatever it is), and I'd like to talk about it. Is that something you're open to?"
"You shouldn't give up. All the hard work will be worth it in the long run."	"It makes sense that you feel that way. This is hard."
(Getting pulled in a new line of discussion when they want to distract you from talking about the issue at hand.)	"That may be true, but I'm talking about this now."
(Jumping in to fix their problem, turning it into your problem in the process) "Let's see what we can do about this."	"Although I don't have a solution for you, I'm looking forward to seeing what you figure out." "I believe in you."
"You're ruining your life. You need to change."	"I'm doing things a little differently. I'm making some changes and wanted to let you know."

Notice almost all of the statements in the "Say this" column start with "I." That's important.

Recovery language is rooted in *your own* recovery. You're stating *your own* truth. You're owning *your own* feelings. You're taking responsibility for *your own* actions. It ties back into figuring out what's yours and what's theirs like I talked about in Chapter 7, and it's one of the keys to not getting caught up in their addiction.

Not only does this allow you to find and keep your own peace but, what's more, it puts you in the empowered position to become a resource for recovery.

Become a Resource for Recovery

The ways to support someone with an addiction are unlike the ways to support someone with any other illness. It's part of what makes addiction so baffling and frustrating for families, because we're wired to care for our loved ones in a certain way when they're sick—with comfort, food, and taking the load off their shoulders. None of that is helpful with addiction. Instead, you inadvertently become a resource for the addiction that you thought you were helping to overcome.

We touched a little in Chapter 3 on one of the biggest ways families contribute to the problem without realizing it: money.

You give your loved one twenty dollars in cash because they tell you they have a speeding ticket, that they need it for an Uber to get to work, or that they need it to buy food so they can eat that day. So, you give it to them.

The thing is you can't know for sure what they're using that money for. The parents of one family I worked with gave their daughter $200 a day, thinking they were helping her because she had told them she needed the money to pay for medication that would help her get sober. That wasn't the case.

I know you don't want to pay a drug dealer money in exchange for your loved one's drugs, but in an indirect way, you may be doing just that by freeing up their dollars so *they* can go buy alcohol and drugs.

I understand how jarring a concept this can be for families to hear. If you don't give your loved one money or pay for these things directly, how will your loved one get to work? Where will they sleep? How will they eat?

Here's the thing though: addicts are some of the most resourceful people in the world. I sure was when I was active. We can find drugs within an hour of being plopped into a new city. We can get alcohol while stuck in a blizzard in the middle of nowhere. We are capable of doing whatever it takes to feed our addictions, which means we are just as capable of getting ourselves to work or finding a way to eat.

We just don't have to worry about doing it for ourselves if we know you are there to do it for us.

You are your loved one's path of least resistance. They *know* how to use you as a resource, so they will continue to turn to you until you make it clear that you are no longer available as a resource for anything but recovery.

One time, a young woman came up to me right after I spoke to a group of patients in a treatment center, and she asked me if she could give me her dad's email address and if I would invite him to my family group. "He enables me, and I know if he doesn't stop, I won't make it."

She was aware of her dad's enabling, but her addiction prevented her from telling him to stop. The likely reason she was able to ask me was that a window of willingness had cracked open in that moment of hearing me speak, allowing the part of her that did want to get better to resonate strongly enough with what I was saying that it was able to rise to the forefront. That window had largely come about by her being in treatment where she was surrounded by recovery. Outside of treatment, it's much easier for the addiction to call the shots.

Money isn't the only way you may be inadvertently acting as a resource for the problem. For instance, what are you supporting emotionally? Are you cosigning the constant chaos and drama of their lives as a result of their addiction? Would you identify as coddling them in their troubles? Being there for someone does not mean that you need to emotionally cosign the drama and chaos that they are in.

Take an honest look at all of it. Really look at where you are putting your time, energy, attention, and resources and ask yourself if it's really been helping or if it's possibly been contributing to the problem instead.

I want to be crystal clear that this is *not* about making you feel bad, placing blame, or creating shame or guilt. This is about opening your eyes so you can (1) stop doing things that aren't helpful, and (2) take new action. If you have those feelings of blame, shame, or guilt, identify them and allow space for them, but then keep moving forward. Those feelings are important for you to process, but you can do that while creating change for you and your loved one.

Through that change, you can learn to become a resource for *recovery*. It's all about doing something different and— you guessed it—walking your own recovery path.

You're most able to become a resource for recovery when you identify your unhealthy loops and take steps to break them. When you identify and detox from what is no longer serving you. When you find your lane and work on staying grounded in it. When you make recovery(love)-oriented decisions rather than addiction(fear)-driven ones.

You're able to become a resource for recovery by making it less possible for addiction to thrive around you.

And you're able to become a resource for recovery by having tools and support on hand to provide to your loved one when they decide they're ready to do something different too: the phone number of a professional they can call who can help them get into treatment (for our clients, this is often myself or one of our case managers or interventionists); the information for a recovery meeting they can go to; the belief in them that they can do this no matter how hard it is, because you've seen what's possible for yourself and for those in recovery.

Those may not initially seem like enough to offer your loved one when you're used to being entangled, but I promise being a resource in this way is far more effective for them and, of course, healthier for you.

Now, this chapter covered a lot of big, heavy things, and it's normal that you might be feeling overwhelmed or nervous at the prospect of changing everything you've been doing. Change in general is uncomfortable, especially when it goes against our natural instincts, so I want to leave you with one last tip.

As you get ready to put into practice the processes outlined in this framework, simply wonder. Ask yourself, "What would it be like for me to not pay for this anymore?" "What might it feel like to not talk to him when he's drunk?" "What might it look like to do something else instead?"

That's it. Be curious and let yourself be open to the possibilities.

KEY CHAPTER TAKEAWAYS

❖ You're currently at a fork in the road. You can keep going down the path you've been traveling of confusion, chaos, and addiction or you can try something different and start down the path of recovery.

❖ Recovery is a forever journey, a way of life. It doesn't end when you reach a certain milestone or achievement.

❖ It's important to note that I'm not teaching you these steps so you can go and teach them to your loved one. That's more of the same loop of trying to rationalize with the addiction, and addiction can't be rationalized with.

❖ Recovery language comes from a place of love rather than fear, but just because it's loving doesn't mean you can't still be angry. It just means you aren't dumping that anger and pain on your loved one.

❖ Your loved one may not respond to you in a loving way (especially not if they're active in their addiction), but over time, their reactions to you will change.

❖ Try using disarming statements and "I" statements to speak from a place of recovery and avoid engaging with the addiction.

❖ The ways to support someone with an addiction are unlike the ways to support someone with any other illness and often go against what our natural instincts say we should do. It's important for us to take a hard look at the ways we may be serving as a resource for the addiction, whether it's financially, emotionally, or otherwise, so we can change our behavior and act as a resource for *recovery* instead.

❖ None of this self-reflection is about creating shame or guilt toward ourselves. It's simply about opening our eyes and taking our heads out of the sand so we can do things differently in order to create lasting change.

CHAPTER 10
FIND YOUR COMMUNITY

I've already mentioned how important community is to recovery, but it's worth mentioning again. Being around people who prioritize their own recovery and who support you in doing the same makes a huge difference, especially early on in recovery. It certainly did for me.

This is not something anyone navigates alone, and I especially recommend getting professional support for both your loved one's sake and your own.

Other ways to get that support are through a fellowship, with a sponsor, and working through the Twelve Steps. (Yes, families can go through the Twelve Steps too. I recommend every single person go through the Twelve Steps at least once in their life.)

I've provided a list of several different fellowship organizations available along with links to their websites where you can find a local or online meeting to attend. You can find the list in the Additional Resources section at the back of this book.

There is no "right" amount of fellowship to get or required number of meetings to attend. You can attend as many or as few as you need; however not all meetings or all fellowship groups are going to be right for all people. I think of it sort of like shopping for clothes. You have to try things on a few times to see how they fit.

When you're first starting out in a fellowship, I recommend going to meetings several times. You don't have to say anything if you don't want to; just go and listen. See if the things being said resonate with you. Or as another phrase I picked up in recovery goes, "Listen for where you're alike." If it resonates, you go back. If after five or six meetings it's not resonating, find another meeting to try instead.

Go to meetings until you want to go to meetings.

If you do choose to work your way through the Twelve Steps, you'll want to do so with guidance from a sponsor.

Finding a sponsor also comes down to listening. Listen to people who are further along in their recovery than you and keep an ear out for someone who has what you want in terms of peace, recovery, tranquility, and serenity. Listen for someone who clearly has access to recovery tools and is comfortable using them. Someone who, as they're talking, you think, "I can't believe they're so calm. I want to be like that." That's the person to approach and ask if they'd be willing to be your sponsor.

Fellowships are only one kind of community that can support you on your recovery journey. I've mentioned finding a therapist or counselor a few times in this book; that's another strong option for a safe container where you can process all your stuff in your lane. If you're religious, church may be where you find community. Yoga and meditation classes are powerful recovery options to consider.

Where you find community isn't as important as how it makes you feel. Look for a community that fills you up and makes it easier to feel grounded in yourself; one that helps quiet the chaos rather than add to it; one where you can witness recovery in action. You'll know it when you find it.

WHAT IS THE BIG BOOK?

Alcoholics Anonymous, also known as the "Big Book," is a book put out by AA that goes through the Twelve Steps and includes personal stories of those who have found recovery in the program. It's an incredible resource for learning about addiction and understanding what it takes to recover.

I strongly recommend that you get a copy of the Big Book to not only read for yourself but to put out on your coffee table so your loved one might see it. This is not so you can preach to them what they should be doing; it's so they can see the work you are putting into your own recovery and know you are a resource they can turn to when they are ready.

To purchase a copy of the Big Book, go here: https://www. aa.org/the-big-book

KEY CHAPTER TAKEAWAYS

- ❖ Community is a crucial element of long-term recovery, and I strongly recommend finding professional support to navigate this process.
- ❖ If you're looking for fellowships, AA, Al-Anon, and ACA are great resources. (A full list of fellowships is in the resource section at the back of this book.)
- ❖ Even if you don't identify as an addict, you can still get a sponsor and go through the Twelve Steps.
- ❖ Other types of community can include finding a therapist, going to church, and finding a yoga or meditation class.

CHAPTER 11
FAMILY SYSTEM INTERVENTION

I f you've made it to this chapter, then you hopefully have a good understanding of how recovering from addiction takes more than someone simply going to treatment. Recovery is a process, and it's one that benefits exponentially from the whole family being involved, especially in creating lasting change. You also now have an idea of some specific changes you can make using the **Dear Family Framework** to begin that process of change for yourself.

While you will see changes when you put this framework into practice on your own, the fastest and most effective way to create the best chance for success for your loved one is to work with a professional.

I'm going to be plainly honest with you: I want you to work with us, and I'm going to use this chapter to explain why. We do things differently, and it has led to unprecedented results. I have witnessed firsthand with our clients the way those differences give you, your loved one, and your family the absolute best chance for long-term recovery success.

If you'd like my team to help you do things differently, too, schedule a call with us here: https://tippingpointrecovery. as.me/connection-call

What Is a Tipping Point Recovery Family System Intervention?

Most people, when they think of an intervention, probably picture a bunch of friends and family standing in a row under a white banner with the word "Intervention" painted on it like in *How I Met Your Mother*. They picture a scary confrontation with the goal of dragging someone to treatment. While an intervention does include a family meeting with your loved one (more on that in a moment), it is so much more than this.

An intervention is not an event. Like recovery, an intervention is a *process*.

For me personally, I feel that an intervention is *any change that is created within a family system*. So, if you're reading this book and making the decision to turn your words, your body, your heart, and your interactions in a different direction, that's a form of intervention.

Just picture dropping a rock in the water and seeing the ripple that goes out. Even the ripple of a tiny pebble goes out pretty far. One small change leads to another and another, and soon your reality is completely different.

A Tipping Point Recovery family system intervention is at a minimum a six-month engagement where we educate, guide, and support you on the journey toward recovery at every stage: before, during, and after your loved one is in treatment.

How Does a Tipping Point Recovery Intervention Work?

There are many interventionists who will promise they'll get your loved one to treatment. They'll spend a day or two or three with you, have a family meeting, and get your loved one into treatment. It's not hard for us professionals to get someone to go to treatment; what is more critical is helping someone to stay in treatment, to commit to a long-term path, to commit to *themselves* for the long term, to stay committed after they return home, and to regain that commitment after they relapse. That's why we at Tipping Point Recovery take a different approach to interventions.

What someone who struggles with drug and alcohol addiction needs is a long-term solution, one where everything and everyone around them understands what it is they need and how to offer healthy help through all the twists and turns this cunning and baffling disease delivers. In order to get a long-term, sustainable solution, there has to be a fair amount of planning and some change within the family system.

Tipping Point Recovery's interventions are customized and comprehensive for just this reason. Each person's recovery journey is different, and so is each family system. What will work for one family won't necessarily work for another, which is why we spend a good amount of time speaking with and educating the family before the meeting with your loved one even takes place. It's also why we continue to provide family support and education during and after your loved one goes into treatment.

It's easy to think that once your loved one goes to treatment, the hard work is done, but this is actually the point where families need the *most* support and even more often don't know where to find it.

Like I said, it's not difficult getting someone into treatment. What's difficult is helping someone to stay in treatment, to accept the help of aftercare, to go into sober living, to manage relapses, to evaluate the next best option, and to stick to a long-term plan. Most families are unprepared to handle what to say and do when their loved one shows up after leaving treatment early or calls to say, "Come pick me up."

We help you navigate all of it. We field the phone calls, mood changes, disagreements, and unpleasantries that are to be expected when someone goes to treatment. We act as a bridge between you and your loved one, as well as you and their treatment center, and we support you through our group program while they're there and beyond.

It's sort of like you're in treatment while they're in treatment. You're learning what they're learning. You're healing as they're healing—you from your lane and them from theirs, walking two parallel recovery paths.

When you hit a bump or a setback (because you both will—recovery can be messy), you will have our group support and professional guidance so you know what to do or say to get back on track.

Throughout this entire six-plus month process, we make sure neither you nor your loved one get dropped.

Again, if you just want your loved one to get to treatment, an intervention with Tipping Point Recovery might not be your thing. If you want your loved to have the absolute best chance of long-term success while you learn how to navigate what arises, how to offer healthy help, how to unpack your own feelings and emotions from what their addiction has left you feeling and thinking, and if you want support along the way, then our interventions are for you!

What If It Doesn't Work?

It's my belief that all our family system interventions work, just maybe not immediately or in the way we initially expect. While in the majority of interventions we do, the person being intervened on does accept the invitation to go to treatment, even the cases where they don't initially accept are not "failures."

It goes back to an intervention being a process and not an event. When you think of it as an event, then if the person says no to treatment the day of the meeting, you think it failed; however, the intervention isn't over there.

I've done interventions where the person being intervened on walked in the front door, saw what was happening, and walked right out the back door without listening to a word of what their family had to say. A few months later, do you know where they were? In treatment.

Because an intervention is a process.

After their loved one walked out the door, I continued to work with that family on setting healthy boundaries, learning how to support only recovery, and finding their own recovery paths, and those changes in the family system eventually led to their loved one being ready to find a path of their own.

Intervention is a process, and sometimes "no" is a part of that process, but hearing "no" doesn't mean the process is over. It means trying one of our other unlimited number of resources to make the change that resonates with the person struggling.

Remember, recovery is about learning to live life without substances. That takes more than just two, three, four, or even twelve weeks of treatment and then coming home. It more often takes a while for someone to latch on to a long-term plan, but an intervention is the start to that plan, and with Tipping Point, it doesn't end there. It's the opportunity for you as a family to start to take back control of the situation.

How do you know if you and your loved one need an intervention?

If you're asking this question, chances are you both need one.

Families tend not to consider interventions because, like with addiction, they don't understand the truth of what interventions are and the power they hold. As someone who has facilitated hundreds of interventions, I can honestly say they have the power to bring miracles. The impact is that great.

I was talking to a woman the other day and suggested an intervention for her loved one. Her response was, "Oh, but he doesn't want to get treatment, and drinking is such a big part of his culture that he probably won't stop."

Neither of those things are reasons to not do an intervention. In fact, they're strong reasons *to* do one, and they certainly have no bearing on whether or not the intervention will work. In my experience, a family system intervention using our framework is more likely to get someone on, and help them stay on, a long-term recovery path than any other thing a family will try. You don't have to wait for the wheels to go off the rails or for it to get "bad enough."

Waiting is often just waiting for it to get worse.

The question is, are you willing to make the change?

KEY CHAPTER TAKEAWAYS

❖ Intervention is a process, not an event.

❖ Tipping Point Recovery's family system interventions are six-plus month engagements that educate, guide, and support you on the journey toward recovery at every stage: before, during, and after your loved one is in treatment.

❖ All interventions work, even if it's not in the way we initially hope for or expect.

❖ If you're asking whether or not you and your loved one need an intervention, the answer is probably yes.

CONCLUSION
WHAT TO DO NEXT?

You've reached the end of this book, and I hope the knowledge and tools you've gained have empowered you to take the next steps you need and want to take.

Here's a quick recap of what we covered:

1. In the first chapters of this book, we took a hard look at the reality you may currently be stuck in as the loved one of someone active in their addiction.

    We looked at how addiction is widely misunderstood, even among medical professionals, and how families tend to self-medicate their pain with anger the same way their loved ones medicate their pain with substances.

    Then, we outlined the three common traps families fall for that prevent them from offering real help to their loved one.

2. Next, we looked at the keys to unlocking a family recovery framework and what specifically about our **Dear Family Framework** makes it so effective.

We also looked at the "frequently made excuses" families make in their own resistance to change and why facing the root of this resistance is so crucial.

3. After that, we dove into the framework itself.

    We talked about how addiction is not about the drugs and alcohol and what the real problem is. We identified the symptoms of what addiction looks and sounds like and the difference between recovery and sobriety.

    From there, we explored finding your own loop and walked through the steps for detoxing from behaviors no longer serving you as a starting point for change.

    Then, I outlined an exercise to help you find and stay in your own lane and gave you a decision-making blueprint to guide you in making recovery-oriented decisions rather than addiction-driven ones.

4. Following that, we covered more ways you can do things differently and take new action, starting with learning a new way to communicate with your loved one.

    We also discussed the importance of assessing the ways you may be serving as a resource for addiction as well as how to go about finding a recovery fellowship.

5. Lastly, we learned about Tipping Point Recovery's family system interventions: what they are, how they work, and why they are so effective for the whole family finding and staying on a recovery path.

The next step for you is simple:

START.

Choose one thing to do differently today than you did yesterday. Tomorrow, pick another, then another. It doesn't matter if they're baby steps or giant leaps as long as they're steps down the path of recovery.

Find your people. Whether that's in our Tipping Point community or a different fellowship, surround yourself with support. Don't try to do this alone. No one recovers alone.

If you decide you would like help from myself and my team, reach out here so we can chat:

https://tippingpointrecovery.as.me/connection-call

We know what you're going through because we've been there. We know how to help your loved one because we've been there too. And we know recovery is possible for both of you because we see it happen every single day.

To doing things differently,

Kate

ADDITIONAL RESOURCES

Included below are various resources I recommend to help you along your recovery journey.

Schedule a Call with My Team

Every family's situation is unique, so our process starts with YOU. Schedule a 30-minute Connection Call for us to hear from you so we can set up a unique plan to get you where you want to be. Whether it's through a family system intervention or one of our other intervention methods, including family system case management and family or loved one-focused recovery coaching, we'll find the help that's right for you.

This 30-minute meeting is for one person or the whole family. It only takes one person to begin the change needed.

Schedule your consultation here: https://tippingpointrecovery.as.me/connection-call

Double Circle Meeting

This is Tipping Point Recovery's online recovery meeting. This meeting is a chance for all those impacted by addiction to come together in community to heal on mirrored paths—both those in recovery from drugs and alcohol and those who identify as family and friends.

Meetings are held every week via Zoom. Sign up here:

https://www.tippingpointrecovery.com/recovery-meeting/

Friends of Tipping Point Online Community

This online community is for people who live with, love, care for, and support people dealing with addiction. Jump in to join the recovery conversations and get access to a plethora of resources within this powerful hub.

Join here: https://www.facebook.com/groups/friendsoftip-pingpoint

Twelve-Step Recovery Fellowships

While this is a list of available twelve-step fellowships, there are many more out there. If you're curious whether a group exists for a specific struggle not listed, I encourage you to search for it online. New groups are created regularly.

Alcoholics Anonymous (AA) — https://www.aa.org/

❖ Meetings are typically listed as "open" or "closed" meetings.

- **Open meetings** are available to anyone interested in the Alcoholics Anonymous program of recovery from alcoholism. Nonalcoholics may attend open meetings as observers. *These are the meetings I recommend family members attend.*
- **Closed meetings** are for AA members only or for those who have a drinking problem and "have a desire to stop drinking."

Al-Anon/Alateen — https://al-anon.org/

❖ For those whose lives have been affected by someone else's drinking. Alateen is specific for young people (mostly teenagers) whose lives have been affected.

Adult Children of Alcoholics (ACA)/Dysfunctional Families — https://adultchildren.org/

❖ A group for people who grew up in dysfunctional homes.

Co-Dependents Anonymous (CoDA) — https://coda.org/

❖ For those who desire healthy & loving relationships.

Narcotics Anonymous — https://na.org/

Nar-Anon — https://www.nar-anon.org/

Learn More About Addiction & Recovery

CCAR — https://ccar.us/

CCAR is a resource for all things recovery and envisions a world where the power, hope and healing of recovery from alcohol and other drug addiction is thoroughly understood and embraced.

National Institute on Drug Abuse (NIDA) — https://nida.nih.gov/

NIDA is the lead federal agency supporting scientific research on drug use and addiction.

Recommended article: Drugs, Brains, and Behavior: https://www.drugabuse.gov/publications/drugs-brains-behavior-science-addiction/drugs-brain

Recovery 2.0 — https://r20.com/

Recovery 2.0 is a global organization dedicated to inspire and unite people in recovery from addiction through the practice of yoga and meditation so that they can heal and thrive.

Videos:

❖ *Everything you think you know about addiction is wrong*, Johann Hari, TED — https://youtu.be/PY9D-cIMGxMs?si=tmx0dJp2jeSBauhx

❖ *Most IMPORTANT video on addiction*, Bruce Lipton & Tommy Rosen — https://www.youtube.com/watch?v=-ka_k49R2GrU

❖ Search "AA Speakers" on YouTube for an unlimited number of powerful stories to inspire hope.

Recommended Reading

On Addiction:

❖ *In The Realm of Hungry Ghosts* by Gabor Maté, M.D.

❖ *Loving Lions* by Michael Wilson

❖ *Recovery 2.0* by Tommy Rosen

❖ *The Big Book* by Alcoholics Anonymous

On Codependency:

❖ *Codependent No More* by Melody Beattie

❖ *Courage to Change* by Al-Anon Family Groups

❖ *Facing Codependency* by Pia Mellody

On Spirituality:

- ❖ *Help, Thanks, Wow: The Three Essential Prayers* by Anne Lamott
- ❖ *Seat of the Soul* by Gary Zukav
- ❖ *Stand Up for Your Life* by Cheryl Richardson
- ❖ *The Four Agreements* by Don Miguel Ruiz

On Trauma:

- ❖ *The Body Keeps The Score* by Bessel A. van der Kolk, M.D.

Learn More About Naloxone

National Institute on Drug Abuse (NIDA) — https://nida.nih.gov/publications/drugfacts/naloxone

Learn about Tapping/EFT (Emotional Freedom Technique)

Tapping 101 — https://www.thetappingsolution.com/tapping-101/

ABOUT THE AUTHOR

Kate Duffy is a Family Addiction Expert and catalyst for change who has been inspiring recovery and healing since she got sober herself in 2013.

After facing and overcoming her own battle with substance use, Kate saw and felt the missing pieces at the recovery initiative tipping point. She has since made it her life's mission to bring families into the recovery conversation. Through hundreds of interventions, Kate has created a proven family-recovery model where families are empowered to rise above the frequency of addiction. When families heal, their loved ones can too.

Kate founded Tipping Point Recovery, Inc. and created the **Dear Family Framework**, a breakthrough approach to recovery that takes a holistic view of the individual within the family system. She now shares this framework nationally so she can help more individuals and their families recover and heal.

Kate knows that successful, long-lasting recovery must bring together the individual, the family, and the treatment facility.

Healing can begin at home.

Learn more about Tipping Point Recovery at our website: https://www.tippingpointrecovery.com/